MANAGING CULTURAL DIVERSITY AT WORK

Khizar Humayun Ansari
and June Jackson

KOGAN
PAGE

First published in 1995

Kogan Page Limited
120 Pentonville Road
London N1 9JN

British Library Cataloguing in Publication Data

A CIP record for this book is available from the British Library.

ISBN 0–7494–1180–5

Typeset by BookEns Ltd., Royston, Herts.
Printed and bound in Great Britain by Clays, St Ives plc

MANAGING
CULTURAL
DIVERSITY
AT WORK

Better Management Skills

This highly popular range of inexpensive paperbacks covers all areas of basic management. Practical, easy to read and instantly accessible, these guides will help managers to improve their business or communication skills. Those marked * are available on audio cassette.

The books in this series can be tailored to specific company requirements. For further details, please contact the publisher, Kogan Page, telephone 0171-278 0433, fax 0171-837 6348.

Be a Successful Supervisor
Business Etiquette
Coaching Your Employees
Conducting Effective Interviews
Consulting for Success
Counselling Your Staff
Creative Decision-making
Creative Thinking in Business
Delegating for Results
Effective Meeting Skills
Effective Performance Appraisals*
Effective Presentation Skills
Empowerment
First Time Supervisor
Get Organised!
Goals and Goal Setting
How to Communicate Effectively*
How to Develop a Positive
  Attitude*
How to Develop Assertiveness
How to Motivate People*
How to Understand Financial
  Statements
How to Write a Staff Manual
Improving Employee
  Performance
Improving Relations at Work
Keeping Customers for Life

Leadership Skills for Women
Learning to Lead
Make Every Minute Count*
Managing Disagreement
  Constructively
Managing Organisational Change
Managing Part-Time Employees
Managing Quality Customer
  Service
Managing Your Boss
Marketing for Success
Memory Skills in Business
Mentoring
Office Management
Productive Planning
Project Management
Quality Customer Service
Rate Your Skills as a Manager
Sales Training Basics
Self-Managing Teams
Selling Professionally
Speed Reading in Business
Successful Negotiation
Successful Telephone Techniques
Systematic Problem-solving and
  Decision-making
Team Building
Training Methods that Work

Contents

Introduction

How to manage a culturally diverse workforce successfully will depend upon a number of factors which relate to the nature of the organisation and the context in which it operates.

An organisation in an area with a culturally heterogeneous population may consider where the staff from different cultural groups are represented in the workforce and at what level in the hierarchy they are working.

A company located in an area populated mainly but not solely by people from one cultural background may draw its workforce exclusively from that culture. The company may wish to ensure that all the people in their catchment area feel that they can apply for jobs in the organisation and are not discouraged from applying because the workforce is all from one particular community.

The factors to be addressed will vary according to the level of current awareness and knowledge of managers and staff, and include the following:

(a) Background to recruitment

Many workforces are unclear about why diversity in the surrounding population is not reflected in their companies. This situation may, in part at least, have arisen from equal opportunities principles not being applied. Even if such principles have been accepted, resistance to the recruitment of people from the excluded groups might arise. Indeed, staff from the traditionally dominant group often believe that staff from other cultural communities have been recruited not on merit or because of their suitability for the job but because of 'positive' (sometimes referred to as 'reverse') discrimination. Their understanding can be that such successful staff are there not on the basis of meeting the selection criteria of the job, but because they received preferential treatment to satisfy equal opportunities laws. This can result in resentment against individuals from these groups. At one end of the spectrum this may cause the breakdown of cooperation among the staff from different cultural backgrounds, and at the other it could lead to a range of forms of discrimination, harassment and victimisation. Either way, the outcomes for the organisation in terms of staff or productivity are unlikely to be beneficial.

(b) Are there language and/or other communication difficulties?

Language issues can become a source of conflict and inequality within culturally diverse organisations. However, as Britain becomes more and more multicultural, especially in light of the push towards greater European integration, our workforce is going to be composed increasingly of people who use English as a second language. And so, accepting and understanding of languages other than English will play an increasingly important part in corporate success. Since English is the predominant language in which business and personal affairs are conducted, organisations need to consider how they can make cross-cultural communication a source of strength.

If staff from particular linguistic groups have little English and this training need is not tackled adequately, natural segregation may arise in the workplace, and this can be difficult to deal with at a later stage. This situation can cause a lack of harmony in the workforce, where messages intended to convey important decisions may reach staff, if at all, in a distorted form; managers not having direct language access to people from other cultural backgrounds may find it difficult to give appropriate feedback or motivate effectively. The non-English speaking staff, on the other hand, may perceive that they are receiving different, and lower quality, treatment and terms and conditions of employment than their English-speaking colleagues.

Alternatively, native English-speaking workers can feel frustrated at the ineffective communication between them and non-English speaking colleagues – in the workplace and socially – and feelings of resentment can build up there.

(c) To what extent and for how long equal opportunities policies have been in place in the organisation

Where an organisation has long had a policy on diversity, there may be a higher level of awareness among staff and greater experience of working in a culturally diverse workforce and the benefits that this can bring. This can lead to a sense of complacency; 'We're OK – we treat everyone the same' and 'I don't notice what colour people are – it's what they do that's important'. In practice, this can mean the imposition of assumptions and values which prevent the recognition of mutual respect among individuals from diverse cultural backgrounds.

Alternatively, it can also lead to a workforce which is more experienced in accepting and valuing differences; and more experienced in working with colleagues from a range of backgrounds.

(d) Has any training been offered to the management and staff?

If there has been an investment in training, staff awareness about the issues of discrimination and disadvantage ought to be heightened. It is important that this training is effective for staff from all cultural backgrounds, and carefully designed to avoid a potential backlash among particular groups. Heightened awareness from training can make for a positive approach to working in a culturally diverse environment; that experience in turn develops the knowledge and skills of staff in working with people of different cultures.

(e) Have changes been introduced to create an environment in which the culturally diverse workforce can perform to its full potential?

For a culturally diverse workforce, changes can be introduced to accommodate and respond to its needs. The extent of any changes and how they have been introduced will affect how successfully the workforce can operate as a team.

(f) The general economic environment in the country

If the general economic environment is poor and unemployment is high, there is more likelihood of resentment building up against employees from groups who are perceived to be marginal, encouraging an atmosphere which is conducive to such comments as 'They're taking our jobs' and 'We're being swamped'.

This book is about the skills required to manage a culturally diverse team effectively. This effectiveness is more likely to be achieved through equal opportunities. The following chapters cover access to employment; training and development; opportunities for promotion; and management skills and styles.

It is important to develop the skills required to manage a culturally diverse team. The manager must begin by considering:

- Access to the organisation;
- The experiences of staff once they are in;
- Factors which then operate against their motivation and progression into the more senior levels.

For the individual, moving into more senior positions means that their influence is greater and the rewards are higher. This increases motivation of both the staff who reach these positions and others from the same cultural background who see positive role models in the organisation. If staff have equal access to senior positions in the organisation, there is more effective use of all the resources available.

CHAPTER 1
Cultural Diversity: Equal Opportunities Transformed?

The subject of cultural diversity in the workplace is highly sensitive and offers a variety of challenges to managers. Effective management of a culturally diverse workforce can mean changes to the working environment, including making a variety of amendments to the current rules and regulations; it also implies the sharing of power and decision-making.

Often individuals will throw up barriers to the changes required by saying that they 'treat everyone the same'. This chapter focuses on the need to move from 'treating everyone the same' towards identifying discrimination, recognising the effects of past discrimination and recognising the exclusion, or under-utilisation, of different sections of society. But much more importantly, a diverse approach means valuing differences and treating people in ways which bring out the best in them.

What is cultural diversity?

Cultural diversity, at the simplest level, reflects the characteristics that may make one individual culturally different from another. Cultural differences involve patterns of lifestyles, values, beliefs, ideals and practices. Cultural diversity includes differences in race, ethnicity, national origin, language and religion.

It is tempting to believe that to learn the details of different cultural norms will help the workforce to operate more effectively. However, learning about different cultures is useful only so long as the dangers of stereotyping are recognised.

A young British woman from a particular cultural or religious background, born and educated in the UK, will have had different life experiences from the older British woman from a similar group, born outside the UK. Age, background, experiences will all have an influence on how the two individuals interact with the culturally dominant population.

Young Asian men, born and educated in the UK, will also have differing influences, pressures and needs from those of older Asian men who have migrated to the UK. And yet, on the face of it, they are from the same ethnic group and gender, and we could be tempted to give a blueprint as to how, for example, a white person should interact with them. This could lead to stereotyping a group rather than finding out about the individual.

The extent of cultural diversity in a given situation depends on the differences of views held about the world, verbal and non-verbal codes of social behaviour, communication styles and expectations of those interacting. To some, it has recently come to mean being different, deviation or divergence from a single standard, specifically that underlying European expectations and ideals – a shift from assimilation towards the creation of separate, confronting identities. To others, it has meant a realisation, celebration and bringing together of what is best in their cultures. For them, it has served as the starting point for enhancement of quality of interactions in the workplace.

So that they can come to grips with changes in the labour market, employers have begun to take a fresh look at the idea of equal opportunities. Instead of resisting it as an imposition from outside, for instance legislation, or as a moral obligation, some are developing new perspectives on how they can harness cultural diversity to become more about 'us' as well as 'them' and so drive the organisation to achieve economic and business goals. More importantly, the focus is beginning to shift away from groups which have been seen as disadvantaged towards individuals and their specific talents. The aim is no longer to remove the differences between groups so that society becomes a melting pot, but to respond to individual merits and aspirations.

The changing nature of the workforce

The effective implementation of equal opportunities in organisations should change the traditional picture of the top tiers of management being almost exclusively white and male. The resulting new mix of staff will create discomfort for some. It is this situation of discomfort which will need to be managed effectively if the company is really going to benefit from the wide range of human resources now available to it.

Attitude formation

Feeling uncomfortable with people who are different and acquiring negative values about them often begins in childhood from a variety of sources, including the family, peers, the community, the school, and the media.

It is important for individuals to reflect on their childhood experiences as these will have influenced later attitudes held in adult life.

Case study
Early experiences

Stage 1
A child comes home from primary school and recites a few words in French to his parents. His parents are delighted at the progressiveness of the school and are impressed at the teaching of a foreign language at such an early stage of the child's education, as they believe that success in the future will lie in being able to communicate in a variety of foreign languages.

Stage 2

A few months later the same child comes home and recites the numbers one to five in Urdu (an Asian language). The parents are furious when they realise that their child is being taught the rudiments of the Urdu language and write to the school to complain and to threaten that they will take their child away if these lessons continue. They contact other non-Asian parents and influence them to take the same action. This causes a rift between the non-Asian and Asian parents.

(a) What is the difference in the parents' reactions in the two stages?
The parents positively accept the European language but are hostile to the Asian one. There is a different value put on the two languages – one valued and the other not. The parents' reaction to the teaching of the Asian language is hostile and aggressive. The strength of this rejection may be based upon a feeling of superiority over a perceived 'inferior' culture of which Urdu is the language.

(b) How might the parents rationalise this reaction to themselves?
The rationalisation for preferring the study of the European language is that it will be more useful for the child in the future, particularly in relation to the workplace. The perception is that, with the 'unification' of Europe, there will be more job opportunities for people who have a command of two, if not more, European languages.

Attempts at justification are often along the lines of 'They're taking over', 'Asian languages will confuse the child – the Asian children will start to use it in school', 'When they come over here they should learn English – our children will be confused and their children will never learn English.' It may not occur to them that acquiring skills in languages of the diverse communities within Britain could help to develop interaction across cultures which could, in turn, have a beneficial effect on relations, not only in the workplace, but also with a wider variety of customers.

(c) Why might they have reacted in this way?
The reaction could be due to the parents' assumptions which evaluate particular cultures and languages negatively. The extreme reactions to the learning of an Asian language would appear to be more to do with their association of Urdu with a people who have often been viewed with disinterest, condescension and perhaps as having little worth.

(d) What attitude might the child now develop towards other cultures?
The child might be adversely influenced by the reaction of the parents. This may turn into holding a negative view of any Asian children in their class and mean that they avoid contact with those children. It is unlikely that the children will mix socially outside school and this could result in losing a valuable opportunity to learn at an early stage about different cultures.

(e) How might this experience of the child affect behaviour in adulthood?
It could lead to a lack of appreciation of other cultures. The attitudes developed in childhood may be transferred in later life into negative attitudes and behaviour in the workplace towards colleagues of different cultural backgrounds. The experience could result in:

- Inability to communicate effectively with people from different cultural backgrounds
- Feeling comfortable only with people of one's own cultural background
- Recruiting and promoting in one's own image − 'cloning'
- Undermining staff from cultures other than one's own
- Avoiding or excluding staff perceived to be culturally different and hence inferior
- Rejecting the principle of valuing differences
- Continued insistence on assimilation
- The possibility that colleagues of different cultural backgrounds may be considered less intelligent and less competent.

Exercise: Influences in one's own childhood

Now consider your own experiences of other cultures in your own childhood:

1. Note any positive images and experiences of other cultures in:

   School: _____

   _____

   _____

   Media: _____

   _____

   _____

   Religion: _____

   _____

   _____

2. Note any negative images and experiences of other cultures in:

   School: _____

   _____

   _____

   Media: _____

   _____

   _____

   Religion: _____

   _____

What influences have any of the experiences you noted on page 16 had for you as an adult?

No organisation can achieve excellence if workers either ignore, perceive as incompetent, or are intolerant of colleagues whose first language is not English. This attitude could be carried into their contact with customers whose first language is not English — with a detrimental impact on customer relations and possible loss of business.

Case study
Language and cultural influences

A company in the service industry has a workforce of 200 personnel. The personnel are a mixture of managers, supervisors, administrative and clerical, catering, cleaning and manual workers.

The company employs people from a wide range of nationalities — particularly from other European backgrounds. The staff from other European countries are mostly Italian and they are exclusively employed in the catering and cleaning work. This situation has been attributed to the language barriers, which do exist. Many of the Italian employees have little English, and certainly not enough to take on office-based work.

The company claims to give a high priority to staff development; however, only one of the Italian workers has ever been promoted into supervisory level work. This experience has not been successful — the Italian supervisor was neither popular with the cleaning staff once she had been promoted nor did she have the skills to deal successfully with the management in her new role. She came across to them as too aggressive. There is discontent among the Italian workers who would like to progress in the company. But, even when opportunities arise to apply for a supervisory position, only the British workers put themselves forward.

The company depends quite heavily on the public sector for its business and, due to pressure from its clients, has recently introduced an equal opportunities policy. This has focused the attention of managers on the obvious division in the workforce and they are keen to address the cause of the problem.

Checklist for action
Senior management:

- Make sure that each member of staff has a job description in their own language, so that lines of authority and reporting are clear.
- Check that staff know about and understand the company's grievance procedures — it may be necessary to produce them in Italian.
- Carry out a training needs analysis; this would probably identify a training need in cross-cultural communication skills across the whole organisation.
- Hold briefings for staff about the specifics and relevance of the newly introduced equal opportunities policy. Hold these briefings in English and Italian, with a question and answer session with managers and supervisors (using an interpreter as required).
- Ensure that staff who are promoted to supervisory level have appropriate skills and have not simply been appointed because they belong to particular cultural groups.
- Provide management and supervisory training for staff promoted into these positions. In particular, for the supervisor in question, provide effective communication skills training.
- Having identified the need for English as a second language (ESL) lessons for the Italian staff, offer appropriate lessons, some in work time.
- Likewise, having identified the need for English supervisors to learn some Italian, offer language classes, some in work time.
- Offer assertiveness skills training to the cleaning and catering staff. It may be necessary to run these in Italian.
- As the company is in the service industry, investigate what languages current and potential clients speak. There may be

a need to use the languages spoken by staff in more creative ways by identifying new markets and improving customer care for particular sections of the market.

The harmonious workplace

Organisations should make the greatest possible use of the human resources available to them. This can only happen in an atmosphere of mutual respect, when all staff benefit from a broader range of experience and viewpoints. The result is a more flexible and effective use of staff and, if a diverse workforce reflects the organisation's market, it can become a more informed, adaptable and productive operation which is closer to the customer and has a competitive edge over less responsive rivals.

Only when the corporate culture is perceived to respond to different needs will individuals from minority cultures be willing to stay and feel that they can succeed; only when jokes which play on stereotypes and demean particular groups no longer generate laughter at the office party will people from diverse cultural backgrounds feel that this is an organisation for them.

Discrimination: myth or reality?

Organisations vary in their responses to cultural diversity in the workplace, ranging from those requiring staff to 'fit in' to traditionally established patterns of values and practices, to those developing ways of tapping individual potential, talents and energy of staff from varied backgrounds.

Furthermore, cultural diversity does not necessarily imply the existence of equal opportunities in the workplace. Indeed, a culturally diverse workforce can result in discrimination against staff from the minority culture, causing discontent and conflict among the workforce and reduction in the organisation's performance and output.

Therefore, without an understanding of the causes and effects of the way that discrimination works, it is unlikely that an organisation can develop policies which are capable of helping managers in their task of managing a culturally diverse workforce effectively. Without a strategy to counter discrimination, there is little likelihood of genuine fairness in treatment of all staff, effective implementation of policies and practices and a fair approach to staff and career development.

In order to identify how discrimination may operate, it is necessary to examine the range of institutional practices in the workplace:

- Recruitment and selection of staff
- Staff training and career development
- Development of a harassment policy and its implementation
- Development of grievance and disciplinary codes
- Introduction of monitoring and evaluation.

Discrimination can be either direct or indirect. In the interpretation of the Race Relations Act and the Sex Discrimination Act, direct discrimination is when one person is treated less favourably than another because of their race, sex or marital status. Indirect discrimination is explained as:

A requirement or condition which is applied equally but a considerably smaller proportion of a particular ethnic group can comply (or it has a disproportionate adverse effect on a particular ethnic group) *and* it is not justifiable.

1. Possible direct and/or indirect racial discrimination
Using recruitment consultants and headhunters is not unlawfully discriminatory. However, it is in how they are used that discrimination may occur.

Direct racial discrimination
If the consultant is cutting out candidates from specific groups at the shortlisting stage this could result in a case of direct racial discrimination.

Exercise: Has discrimination occurred?

Consider the following and decide if you think direct or indirect discrimination has occurred or could occur in each situation:

1. A company uses recruitment consultants and headhunters for all its recruitment.

   Your response: _____

   _____

   _____

2. A Pakistani job applicant is appointed rather than a white job applicant to get more of a mix in the team.

   Your response: _____

   _____

   _____

3. Fifteen years' work experience in the UK is required for senior professional posts.

   Your response: _____

   _____

   _____

4. Irish applicants are not appointed because the manager has had problems in the past with Irish members in the team.

   Your response: _____

   _____

   _____

Indirect racial discrimination

The issue here is what information about their equal opportunities policy and objectives the company includes in the brief to the consultants. Some consultants will be active in terms of equal opportunities; but, this is by no means standard and should not be taken for granted. If the company currently has few or no minority ethnic employees, and no clear instruction is given in the brief to the consultants, they may receive a subtle message about who would and would not 'fit' in that company, and recruit accordingly.

2. Possible direct racial discrimination against the white applicant

'Mix of the team' (in effect, quotas, which are unlawful under the Race Relations Act) does not justify racial or sexual discrimination. The only exemption is under the 'genuine occupational qualification' clause – when race (or gender) is specifically required to carry out the job (for example one-to-one personal counselling, attention of a personal nature, or for reasons of authenticity in a restaurant).

The example given is of a person being appointed purely on grounds of their ethnic origin. This could be deemed to be discrimination in reverse. The example demonstrates that the race relations legislation supports both the minority *and* the majority ethnic group. However, in practice it is often the person from the culturally dominant group who gets the job in order to 'balance the team', that is, to ensure that areas do not develop in the workplace which are staffed exclusively by minority ethnic staff which may be perceived by management to create an intimidatory environment for staff from the majority culture. This would equally be considered direct racial discrimination.

3. Possible indirect racial discrimination

This requirement could well have a 'disproportionate' effect on minority ethnic people. The question here is justifiability. If challenged, the company will be required to justify the length of UK experience asked for, and is unlikely in most instances to be able to justify the requirement.

In many cases this kind of discrimination is 'unintentional', because of inherited practices which have not been thought about in terms of their impact.

4. Direct racial discrimination

This could be direct discrimination on racial grounds.

This does happen, of course, though it may not come to light because reasons other than nationality are put forward for an applicant being unsuccessful. If managers do not have the awareness and the skills to operate effectively within a mixed team then this kind of reaction is the only option they feel there is available to them to deal with their work situation.

From assimilation to diversity

We often see discrimination that results unintentionally from treating individuals and groups which are culturally diverse as if they were homogeneous. A common understanding of equal opportunities is that it means 'treating everyone the same'. In this view there is no need to alter treatment to embrace all the cultural variables.

For example, a social event held for employees and their families may be the managing director holding a cheese and wine party for staff and their families. The entertainment provided may be European classical music. Everyone is being provided with the same entertainment; however, in an organisation with a diverse workforce this environment may result in staff with particular cultural and religious affiliations feeling 'foreign' and therefore uncomfortable. The company would do well to include aspects of the cultures represented in this workforce by offering a range of food and music.

The problem with a 'colour blind' approach and other forms of ignoring diversity is that they deny variation in people's real-life experiences and significant aspects of their identities. Advocacy of a monocultural workplace may serve to condone and maintain institutional barriers to access, status, power, resources and benefits, such as:

- Exclusion from decision-making bodies
- Being overlooked for career development opportunities
- Receiving information through the 'grapevine'.

These barriers in turn have an adverse impact on employees' lives. The notion of the 'same' treatment assumes adherence by all to the 'norm' — that which is expected and happens most often, given a specific set of conditions. What is different or deviates from the norm becomes 'abnormal'. That which members of groups consider normal is patterned by culture, class and time. Therefore, if real equality of treatment is desired, with equality in terms of positive outcomes for all the individuals working for an organisation, then the 'same' treatment may not help us to achieve this.

Consider the following: two Pakistani operatives from the paint-shop are disciplined for breaking health and safety regulations. Their offence was warming up food on a camping-style stove on the line. The two operatives argue that they were forced to bring food and warm it up on the line because their request for halal food in the canteen has produced no response.

It can be argued that since the same rules would be applied to every employee in this case no discrimination has taken place. These rules are likely to have been formulated when the workforce was homogeneous and the rules met their needs. Clearly, these rules have become inadequate in the multi-cultural context since they have come to conflict with the needs of a specific group of workers. It is also true that the existing regulations in practice seem to have a detrimental effect on one ethnic group and can therefore be deemed to be indirectly discriminatory against them. With this in mind, the idea of 'equal quality of treatment' has developed, where different access and treatment is more likely to deliver equal opportunities in employment and services. To bring this about, a review of hitherto accepted procedures may be necessary. But, more importantly, to get the most out of people who come from different cultural backgrounds to their own, managers will need to understand and appreciate these differences. In this case the manager could do the following:

- Carry out a survey of dietary requirements in order to develop the provision made in the canteen
- Provide a room where staff with specific dietary requirements could heat up their own food
- Provide halal meat periodically in the canteen and evaluate take-up
- See if the provision of vegetarian food would be an acceptable compromise and evaluate take-up; there is likely to be take-up of a vegetarian option by other staff.

If an organisation has historically drawn its workforce from a monocultural population, the rules and regulations (written and unwritten) will probably have been developed correspondingly. In the culturally diverse community of the UK, with the move towards a workforce in which there is to be less segregation and more equitable relationships, some of the old rules and regulations are being challenged – sometimes internally and sometimes externally – and supported by the provisions of anti-discrimination legislation.

Case study
Tradition and corporate image

In the transport sector, where there are employees from a wide range of cultural backgrounds, a large number of staff are in jobs which require a company uniform.

A city bus company is introducing a new uniform to enhance the corporate image. The instructions are that staff wearing the company uniform must wear the regulation uniform cap which is issued with the jacket and trousers. After a discussion within the senior management team, an exception is made of Sikh men (of whom there are reasonable numbers) who will be allowed to wear their turbans. Sikh men in a number of other companies have been wearing turbans as part of their uniform and the management therefore do not consider that this will be too contentious an issue. However, the management recognise that some of the rest of the staff may resent the exception being made. The management agree with the Sikh male staff that turbans in the company colours is an acceptable compromise.

However, there is still a negative reaction from a number of the other men, who until now have been allowed to wear their own headgear. They argue that they too should be allowed to wear any kind of headgear as long as it is in the company colours. They perceive the exception for the Sikh men to be preferential treatment and unfair to the other staff, primarily the white staff.

(a) Do you consider that the change of rule for Sikh men is undue preferential treatment?
Sikhs are recognised as an ethnic group; the turban is accepted as one of the key symbols of Sikh culture and is generally required to be worn by practising Sikh men. This adaptation of uniform rules is allowed for within the Race Relations Act in recognition of their religious and cultural needs. A uniform requirement which insists that Sikh men remove their turban has been considered to be unlawful indirect racial discrimination because of its adverse impact on their employment opportunities.

The benefit to the organisation of reviewing this kind of requirement is that the change will help to attract a wider range of applicants and create an image of an organisation which is sensitive and flexible in its approach to employment practices and genuinely inclusive of cultural diversity. Such an organisation would appear to be focused on individual merit and prepared to remove barriers which get in the way of its objectives of recruiting and retaining the most skilled and talented people.

The following are examples of other criteria which may be discriminatory.

- Length of residence in the UK (based on the assumption that 'they need to know the British standards and ways we do things here')

- Requirements for UK qualifications
- Higher language requirements than are necessary for the job to be carried out
- Stipulation about which areas of a city applications will or will not be accepted from.

Any of these criteria may be written or unwritten.

(b) Is it fair and lawful to allow this one exception for Sikh men?
The Race Relations Act and its interpretation is a reflection of Britain as a multicultural society and an attempt by society to work towards *integration*, in other words the process in which all people are offered equal opportunity and mutual respect in the context of cultural diversity.

Checklist for action

- Pre-empt any resistance rather than allow it to emerge — brief staff before the change is introduced.
- Brief the workforce in good time about the planned uniform changes.
- Include in the briefing information the business reasons for the change — linking it to the company's image, profitability and therefore financial survival.
- Give details about the styles of uniform which will be available.
- Explain any exceptions or new introductions, eg for reasons of gender, disability, race or religion. Place these exceptions within the context of the image which the organisation is projecting to its current and potential customers who are also from a variety of backgrounds.
- Allow for questions and answers.

How are other cultures regarded?

There are still plenty of organisations in which different value is put on other cultures. Although this value can be positive or negative, often the tendency is to view events from the perspective of one's own culture. This generally means that other cultures tend to be undervalued and considered inferior compared with one's own. As a result of this devaluing, individuals from other cultural backgrounds are judged negatively and their contribution is also assessed to be of less value and therefore deserving fewer rewards.

Exercise: Assess your own organisation

		Yes	No
1.	Staff from all cultural backgrounds are well integrated in the organisation and are represented at all levels.	☐	☐
2.	Information has been collected regarding uniform requirements, canteen facilities, and there is recognition of non-Christian festival days, in order to plan for the needs of all staff.	☐	☐
3.	Company literature projects a positive image of a multicultural working environment.	☐	☐
4.	The organisation has collected information about the range of languages spoken by staff so that they can be called upon if required by customers.	☐	☐

What action could you take to develop any of the above in your organisation?

The fear of preferential treatment

Many staff from culturally 'marginal' backgrounds come into an organisation with experience of discrimination. To create an environment in which there is mutual respect and understanding which leads to effective teamworking, it is vital to consider how employees' access to opportunities, resources, information and treatment in the workplace will help.

This issue can only be challenged if the managers are proactive and are seen to pay attention to fairness in their day-to-day interactions with staff. The managers' lead needs to be supported by company policy and procedures, and these must be effectively communicated to all staff.

However, because of the sensitivity of openly discussing concerns about fairness in a multicultural workplace, the related issues are not easily aired. There is often, therefore, a lack of knowledge or misinformation and ignorance about the organisation's policy on cultural diversity and what it is trying to achieve. Any attempt to break from the 'same treatment' response is in danger of being perceived as offering preferential treatment or reverse discrimination and therefore unfair treatment against the majority group. Managers need to be aware of this possibility when attempting to introduce greater sensitivity to cultural differences within the workplace.

In the following exercise consider to what extent you would be able to respond to the person making each of the statements.

Exercise: Preferential treatment?
Do you agree or disagree with each statement? Could you hear it said in your own organisation or team?

	Agree	Disagree	Could hear it said in own organisation
(a) You can't say what you think these days without someone saying that you're being offensive.	☐	☐	☐
(b) They've got a chip on their shoulder (said of people from minority cultures).	☐	☐	☐
(c) Equal opportunities is for them, not for me (ie for minority cultures).	☐	☐	☐
(d) I don't notice anyone's colour – why are we making such a big deal of it?	☐	☐	☐
(e) They (people from other cultural backgrounds) come over here, take our jobs, and now they want us to change our rules, regulations and customs for them.	☐	☐	☐
(f) I don't mind as long as I don't have to work for one.	☐	☐	☐
(g) When in Rome do as the Romans do.	☐	☐	☐
(h) They should speak our language when they are at work – it's rude to speak foreign languages in front of English people – they're probably talking about us.	☐	☐	☐
(i) There couldn't be racial discrimination in an organisation which employs a high number of minority ethnic staff.	☐	☐	☐

(a) You can't say what you think these days without someone saying that you're being offensive.
Agreement may indicate:

- Monocultural assumptions are held, and it is acceptable to express these views in the organisation.
- Staff and managers may be concerned about being thought of as culturally insensitive.
- Staff and managers may be concerned that there are certain things that cannot be said — that there is 'politically correct language'.
- The speaker has had a previous bad experience of being accused of prejudice (either a justified or unjustified accusation).
- There is a lack of effective cross-cultural communication skills.
- There is a lack of ability to perceive the issues from another cultural perspective.
- There is a lack of openness in debating the issues.
- There is an unwillingness to acknowledge that we can all make mistakes in cross-cultural interaction.

(b) They've got a chip on their shoulder.
Agreement may indicate:

- An assumption that staff from minority cultures will always make complaints and jump to the conclusion that discrimination is happening when it is not.
- That the work environment is such that staff from culturally diverse backgrounds may not get appropriate feedback from managers.
- A lack of understanding and awareness of the range of experiences of people from minority cultural backgrounds which may justifiably generate intense reactions.

(c) Equal opportunities is for them, not for me.
Agreement may indicate:

- A lack of understanding of equality principles.
- Either a lack of information or wrong information being disseminated about the organisation's policy.
- Resentment of colleagues or superiors who are culturally different.
- Equal opportunities being implemented inconsistently.

(d) I don't notice anyone's colour — why are we making such a big deal of it?
Agreement may indicate:

- A lack of understanding and appreciation of how direct and indirect discrimination operate in an organisation.
- A 'colour-blind' or 'culture-blind' approach, ignoring specific concerns and needs.

(e) They come over here, take our jobs, and now they want us to change our rules, regulations and customs for them.
Agreement may indicate:

- Resentment of any migrant workforce.
- Assumption that 'we' have more rights than 'them'.
- View that anyone from a culture other than one's own 'doesn't belong'. Lack of recognition of the UK as a culturally diverse nation.
- Ignorance of the history of migration, which shows that migration is a global phenomenon and people who migrated to the British Isles from around the world were in many instances invited to fill the vacancies at the lowest rung vacated by the 'native' population, who had opportunities to take up better jobs.

(f) I don't mind as long as I don't have to work for one.
Agreement may indicate:

- Resistance to staff from marginal cultures, and managers in particular.
- Resentment of staff from minority cultural backgrounds moving up the hierarchy, the assumption being that their 'natural' place is that of a subordinate.
- A view that staff from minority cultures are inherently inferior.

(g) When in Rome do as the Romans do.
Agreement may indicate:

- View that people need to 'fit in' on the terms set by people from the majority culture – that there can be no give and take.
- Misinformed view that people who migrate to different countries necessarily give up all their values, traditions, habits, and social and cultural ways to 'fit in' with the majority culture.
- Misinformed view that people who are culturally different from 'us' have come from 'somewhere else'.
- Assumption that everyone in a society agrees and conforms to a fixed set of standards.

(h) They should speak our language when they are at work – it's rude to speak foreign languages in front of English people – they're probably talking about us.
Agreement may indicate:

- View that other cultural groups talk about the majority group in derogatory ways.
- View that the workplace should operate exclusively in one language, regardless of the linguistic backgrounds of staff.
- Resentment of people being different.
- View that people need to 'fit in'.
- Genuine concern that there will be no adequate communication unless there is a common language.
- Lack of awareness of the material reasons why 'they' may be unable to speak in 'our' language.

- Lack of inclination to develop effective strategies for cross-cultural communication.

(i) There couldn't be racial discrimination in an organisation which employs a high number of minority ethnic staff.
Agreement may indicate:

- View that numbers are all that matter.
- Assumption that because ethnic minorities are recruited into the organisation there will be no discrimination in relation to promotion or development opportunities.

Exercise: Identification of differential treatment

1. In your broad experience of the working environment, what practices can you identify which may result in differential treatment, either directly or indirectly, against people who are from minority cultures?

2. What could be done to stop such practices?

CHAPTER 2
Overcoming Resistance and Gaining Ownership

The shift from treating everyone the same to accepting and valuing differences within the work team requires a process of individual and organisational change.

This change is viewed either as an adjustment to external and internal pressures or as an initiative anticipating future developments, but the main objective is still to increase the effectiveness and competitiveness of the organisation.

A shift is required not only in the cultural environment of the organisation but also in:

- Individual values, attitudes and behaviour
- An increase in individual awareness and knowledge
- Development of individual skills to communicate effectively in a culturally diverse team.

However, if the team is becoming more mixed in terms of cultural background, there may be resistance to the changes as familiar social structures and relationships disappear. Ambiguity and uncertainty become increasingly painful and threatening, thereby triggering defensiveness and giving rise to hostility and resentment.

Resistance to change tends to emerge in situations where there is no perceived advantage. For example, there is rarely staff resistance to a salary increase or to increased office space or other rewards, but there is often resistance or a challenge when redundancies are on the cards or when an office move is imposed.

Barriers to achieving change

In order to manage cultural diversity at work effectively, there needs to be an awareness of the potential barriers to the process of change. These barriers can be personal, organisational or environmental. They can stem from the majority, or traditional group, who are resisting change and from the minority, or non-traditional group, who have to work out strategies to operate within the majority culture.

This chapter gives examples of the barriers which the manager can face in developing a high-performing culturally diverse team and includes suggestions on overcoming the barriers.

Individual and attitudinal barriers
You might include:

- Lack of knowledge, awareness or understanding of equal opportunities issues and principles
- Prejudice and stereotypes (particularly negative) about other cultural or racial groups
- Lack of commitment
- Lack of involvement
- Lack of confidence
- Apathy and inertia
- Fear of the unknown; of appearing incompetent; of losing power to cultural groups or individuals from such groups perceived to be traditionally subordinate; of sharing power with individuals from different cultural backgrounds – all resulting in defensiveness
- Social and cultural conditioning
- Self interest – minority individuals seen as threats to dominance, material privilege, job security and career progression

Exercise

Consider what barriers there may be to developing a high-performing culturally diverse work team in your organisation. Some examples are given on pages 36 and 38–43.

Individual and attitudinal barriers	Interpersonal barriers (behaviour towards others)	Structural, environmental, and organisational barriers

- Anxiety at perceived threats to job security, etc
- Degree of discomfort with something or someone that is different
- Denial that discrimination poses any problem; that cultural difference is an important part of social interaction
- Belief that all people are the same, with similar values, attitudes, assumptions, problems, needs and objectives.

To take some examples of these barriers:

Lack of awareness of equal opportunities issues and principles
'I know there are people who think that the organisation should hand them a good job because of their race'; 'Just to promote a coloured person doesn't do them or us any good'; 'The company is so busy trying to be fair to those from the ethnic minorities that it is neglecting the average white male which is discrimination in reverse.'

Prejudices and stereotypes
'Asians are only interested in money ... they prefer to work in their own business ... they tend to work to a large degree among their own people ... they are more numerate, hardworking and conscientious than Afro-Caribbeans who are lazier and lack the work ethic'; 'Bright Asians go into professions not industry'; 'Afro-Caribbeans lack business ethic'; 'Jews go into money-lending'; 'Irish people are all labourers.'

Apathy and inertia
'I don't see what the problem is.'

Self-interest – minority individuals seen as threat to dominance, material privilege, job security and career progression
'They create a lot of their own problems; once they are promoted, they try to pull only their brothers up.'

Belief that all people are the same, with similar problems, needs and objectives
'I don't see why you should treat one individual differently

from another ... if I asked for extended leave it would be rejected but if they wanted a holiday in India they would be granted it.'

Interpersonal barriers
You may have included:

- Showing annoyance at behaviour that differs from that of the majority cultural group
- Patronising behaviour — while giving the impression that the relationship is of equals, in reality a sense of social and cultural dominance is maintained through power imbalance
- Avoidance of contact
- Pressure to conform
- Lack of participation
- Lack of cross-cultural communication skills — different perceptions of degree of eye contact, different interpretations of body language, degree of directness, degree of challenging or obstruction, degree of formality
- Conflict of interest and confrontation
- Lack of trust.

To take some examples of these barriers:

Showing annoyance at behaviour that differs from that of the majority cultural group
'They tend to speak in their own language when they walk in and that tends to annoy people.'

Patronising behaviour
'It is incumbent on white people to be nice to black people and there should be more integration.'

Avoidance of contact
'I find it difficult to understand Jamaicans and Asians with their heavy accents, and tend to avoid working with them.'

Structural, environmental and organisational barriers
You may have included:

- Lack of cultural diversity in the staff mix
- Lack of opportunities for individual development
- Low morale
- Absence of role models
- Low reward or incentive for initiatives promoting cultural diversity
- Marginalisation of a new idea, policy or practice
- Tokenism and palliatives
- Insufficient or inaccurate information about the organisation's policies and goals
- Lack of understanding about the reasons for equal opportunities change, its nature and its likely impact
- Economic climate
- Management structures
- Inappropriate leadership style
- Lack of top management commitment and support for pluralistic initiatives
- Existing systems
- Established practices
- Organisational culture entrenched in ethnically homogeneous relationships and arrangements established over time
- Preference for status quo and aversion to risk-taking
- Incompatibility of pluralistic change with existing systems, procedures, traditions and conventions
- Low tolerance of change
- Imposed/unplanned change – discouraging ownership leading to dissatisfaction
- Unclear objectives
- Inadequate feedback systems and poor communication and consultation mechanisms
- Quick pace of pluralistic change leaving little time for absorption and consolidation; reinforcing uncertainty and instability inherent in such change
- Resource constraints adversely affecting the delivery of a

programme of cultural diversity
- Lack of long-term planning to integrate equal opportunities into the organisation through, for example, incorporating this subject into the annual training programme
- Unequal burdens — different levels, types, and experience of racial/cultural discrimination for staff from non-traditional backgrounds
- Pressure to discriminate from other sources — media, politicians, customers and public.

To take some examples of these barriers:

Insufficient or inaccurate information about the organisation's equal opportunities policy
'By highlighting cultural diversity it produces resentment.'

Lack of understanding about the reasons for equal opportunities, its nature and its likely impact
'The company does employ ethnic minorities, but with more there could be a problem'; 'Such an attitude would itself encourage bias against ethnic minorities in recruitment and lead to unofficial 'quotas' being instituted.'

Economic climate
'During an economic recession, equality issues can often be considered to be a luxury, resulting in training on the subject being cut. This is also a time when prejudices can re-emerge, with ethnic minority staff being the ones to be laid off first.'

Lack of commitment
'I do not know if it (equal opportunities) would make any difference ... personally I am against such things. It is the wrong way of going about it ... my fear is that it is going to be cosmetic.'

Organisational culture entrenched in culturally homogeneous relationships and arrangements established over time
'There have been instances of ethnic minority candidates who

have been rejected although they have exactly the same qualifications, if not better than those selected'; 'The personality of the candidate is very important ... we also look for sociability and assess whether a person will fit in with the company atmosphere'; 'Customers expect a conventional appearance. Dreadlocks are out in sales. We are in an industry of smart suits ... image is important.'

Incompatibility of equal opportunities change with the existing systems, procedures, traditions and conventions
'If we change the nature of the organisation and have procedures for positive action, this would be strange to the culture of this organisation.' (For an explanation of *positive action*, see the glossary on page 127.)

Established practice
'We use our informal network to secure our staff requirements'; 'It is the policy of the company to give preference, insofar as recruitment is concerned, to the relatives of employees.'

Institutional discrimination
'There are set holidays during the year – with extra time at Christmas. We don't automatically allow staff to take time off for other religious festivals during the year; just the national ones at Christmas and Easter'; 'Potential is identified through individual managerial judgement. We don't have a formal appraisal system.'

Pressure to discriminate from other sources
'Cultural diversity in the company could upset the market place. The company is sales and services orientated, therefore we mirror our client ... customers may not want a coloured person. It has occurred that a customer did not want to speak to a black person.' 'I have customers ring and ask for no blacks and no women.'

The case studies in this chapter demonstrate individual and environmental barriers and how they operate. Each of the cases demonstrates elements of either the individual or environmental barriers which are listed above.

Resistance to change is demonstrated in a variety of ways ranging from clinging on to the old ways, to outright hostility to the new. The following case study shows an extreme reaction to the changing workplace which requires an appropriate response if there is to be effective integration in a culturally diverse workforce.

Case study
Manager from a minority culture managing a workforce from the majority culture

John is of Afro-Caribbean origin. He has reached middle management level in his company and now manages a department of 30 staff (all white). He is the first black member of staff to reach this level of management and is consequently the most senior member of staff from a minority group in the organisation.

John has recently had cause to discipline a member of his staff. On his arrival at his office on the day after the disciplinary meeting, John found that obscene and racist graffiti had been sprayed on to the walls and over the files and papers on his desk.

(a) What are possible sources of conflict in this case?
There may be many sources of conflict located in emotions, values and needs. The following may be some of those present:

- Lack of acceptance of the Afro-Caribbean manager's authority; perceived abuse of power based on the staff's assumption that minority managers are unable to handle power and instead use it for its own sake.
- Perceived infringement of the rights of individual staff.
- Rejection of the minority manager's ability to make the correct judgement; perceived inability of a minority manager to apply an appropriate punishment.

(b) What has provoked this reaction in his staff and his colleagues?
This reaction could be provoked by a feeling of being
threatened by the action of an 'uppity black'. The white
subordinate staff feel powerful as part of the dominant culture.
They may expect collusion and support from further up the
organisational hierarchy. This perception results in the
assertion of group power which, it is hoped, will put this
'outsider' in his place.

There could be resistance to a perceived change in the
balance of power — a reaction from the staff belonging to the
majority culture to being in a position where the power was
now being exercised by the individual from a minority group
not previously associated with power.

There could also be a perception that the manager's action
stems from incompetence, which might be presumed to be a
characteristic of all minority managers.

The white members of staff (and possibly management
colleagues) feel the need to signal that they will not accept
criticism or correction, about themselves or a colleague, from a
minority manager.

*(c) What are the potential costs to the company of the above
situation?*
If the company were not to take appropriate disciplinary
action, and to put in place measures to try to stop this kind of
incident happening again, an industrial tribunal would very
likely find it to be a case of unlawful direct racial
discrimination.

Checklist for action
Action for the minority manager to take.

- Assess carefully whether this is an instance of which you
  want to make an issue or one that you would rather avoid
  or ignore.
- Recognise the pressure of being a minority manager and
  avoid unreasonable blame for difficulties.
- Talk with other managers — both from minority and

majority backgrounds — about skills, information and resources which can be brought to bear on this problem.

- Take a problem-solving approach: review all the facts and identify the underlying causes of the problem; discuss various solutions; negotiate a resolution which is perceived in everybody's interest and for which ownership is accepted.
- Ask yourself whether you wish to confront the whole team with the issue or whether working with and influencing individuals would furnish a more effective resolution — either way make sure that there is no loss of face or dignity.
- Choose the appropriate mode of conflict resolution to fit the case in hand; apply calmness, tact and sensitivity in meetings handling such awkward cases.

Action for the organisation and senior management to take. The following are suggestions for action by the organisation. The most important issue is to check first with the individual who is on the receiving end of this treatment in order to agree any action to be taken.

Short-term

- Call a meeting of the team in which this incident has occurred to inform them of what has happened and that the incident is being investigated.
- Make a clear statement to the team that this behaviour will not be tolerated.
- Carry out a full investigation to identify the culprit.
- If the culprit is found, follow the company's disciplinary procedures, which could lead to dismissal.
- Ensure that the individual who has been treated in this way can continue to carry out duties.

Long-term

- Ensure that minority managers are not cast in the role of tokens, in other words in jobs which do not match their skills or experience and therefore set them up for failure.

- Ensure that minority managers are not excluded from useful informal and formal networks; recognise their isolation and offer support to overcome it.
- Recognise difference in the power that managers from majority and minority cultures are perceived to have and the ways in which it can be equalised.
- Introduce or re-launch the company's policy and procedures on harassment.
- Brief all employees on what the policy means in practice, including how they can bring a grievance forward.

Common causes of harassment

Policies often include at least those issues covered in legislation, namely race and sex, but go beyond those elements to other areas such as sexual orientation. A policy may indicate that harassment can happen on the grounds of:

- Race, ethnic origin, nationality or skin colour
- Sex or sexual orientation
- Religious or political beliefs
- Willingness of the individual to challenge harassment, leading to victimisation
- Membership, or non-membership, of a trade union
- Physical, mental or learning disabilities
- Ex-offender status
- Age
- Actual or suspected infection with AIDS/HIV.

Recruitment policies and cultural diversity

Attempts to bring about a change in the composition of the workforce can, if ineffectively carried out, produce further barriers which then need to be overcome. The following case study explores the issue of positive action in recruitment and the backlash which this can have in the organisation if it is not managed effectively.

Case study
The backlash

In a small local council office, based in a culturally diverse area, one member of a team of workers leaves. All the team members are white. The manager decides to take the opportunity to try to attract applicants from the widest possible cross-section of the multicultural population in the organisation's catchment area. This measure is taken as part of the strategy to:

- Broaden the pool of skills and talents from which to draw the workforce
- Project a more diverse image in order to create a greater identification with the community which it serves
- Communicate to the whole community its commitment to meeting their needs
- Encourage greater use of its services by all sections of the community.

The first stage is to ensure that none of the selection criteria is directly or indirectly discriminatory.

Once this is done, the vacant position is advertised in the press, including the minority press, and information is distributed to individuals and organisations who might be interested in the opportunity, or know someone who would be interested. The advertisement and further particulars include a statement positively welcoming applications from all sections of the multicultural community.

The successful applicant is an Asian man. A couple of weeks into the job, he begins to feel the resentment of colleagues. They help new white colleagues but do not extend that help to him. He also overhears someone saying that he got the job because he was given preferential treatment as a minority applicant, to the detriment of other applicants.

(a) What had the manager been trying to achieve?
The manager was aiming at creating a more diverse team.

Perhaps he was trying to counteract the effects of past discrimination and disadvantage through positive action, as recommended in legislation. The manager may have been attempting to break the mould and have seen the initiative as a start to developing a diverse team — the manager's contribution to quality management leading to a value for money service.

(b) What went wrong and why?
The perception of some of the staff is that positive discrimination has occurred and that the Asian applicant has been appointed because of his ethnic origin, not because of his ability to do the job. This was clearly not what was intended nor is it lawful under the Race Relations Act. Discrimination *in favour* of a person on the grounds of race or ethnic origin is unlawful.

The staff seem not to have understood the distinction between positive action and positive discrimination. Positive action recommends special training and encouragement but nevertheless requires selection on the basis of merit. Positive discrimination implies quotas for specific racial or ethnic groups. The institution seems not to have disseminated the relevant information about the distinctions between these two ideas, thus causing resentment. Some may feel that the organisation is wanting 'to be seen' to implement its policy on cultural diversity, but in fact is being tokenistic.

Tokenism is the practice of offering opportunities to individuals from minority ethnic groups not necessarily on the basis of merit but as representatives of ethnic groups. The intention is to give the impression that discrimination does not occur on ethnic grounds. The main criterion on which individuals from minority ethnic groups are given consideration is not competence or capability but ethnic origin. This practice has the effect of producing a backlash among white employees from other ethnic backgrounds (similar to that produced in men if women are on the receiving end of this practice).

Also, measures to create cultural diversity come to be

viewed as reverse discrimination by staff who believe that such steps are not addressed to them nor are they intended for their benefit. Indeed, they perceive themselves to be excluded from the benefits of such actions.

Tokenism also reinforces existing racial stereotypes, if the person appointed has in fact not been appointed on merit, with the skills to do the job, and is therefore not able to carry out the job successfully. The impact on the person recruited is reduced confidence and self-esteem. It also affects their relationship with colleagues from other cultural backgrounds who perceive that the employee has had preferential treatment.

Checklist for action

- Before taking positive action in recruitment, consider carefully the reasons for doing so. Ensure that the reasons link to the company's aims.
- Ensure that the job is advertised internally as well as externally; be clear what objectives are likely to be achieved by using the different channels, including the minority press.
- Share information clearly with staff about why the positive action statement is being made in the advertisement. Methods of sharing the information will vary according to the communication style generally adopted in the company and according to the size of the team. However, it should be possible to:

    —Circulate a written brief explaining positive action.
    —Hold a briefing meeting with the team.

- Ensure that your staff are aware that people of all cultural backgrounds can apply.
- If the successful applicant is from a minority group ensure that their induction period is being set up in the same way as for all other staff. Consider selecting one of the other staff to ensure that the new worker is included in the team.
- Double-check directly with the new worker how he or she is integrating into the team, and check how the team is evolving in the changed situation.

Exclusion zones

The everyday organisation of the workplace and the world outside within which it operates can create situations which are unfair for staff whose cultural background is different from that of the majority of workers. The following case studies explore environmental factors which can operate as barriers to all employees contributing to their maximum capacity.

Case study
Lack of integration

Consider the following situations:

Situation I
An Asian man in a group of white colleagues does not participate in the social side of work; lunching together in the canteen and drinking in the bar after work.

Situation II
A group of women of African origin sit together every day at lunch, speaking in their first language (an African language).

(a) Why might these situations arise?
Situation I
This behaviour may be due to the 'exclusionary' attitude of the white colleagues. The Asian employee may feel that he is being excluded from the informal network. The majority group could be indicating that they do not expect him to join their group, thus reducing him to the status of an observer.

The Asian employee may not share the common interests of the white colleagues which are discussed at length at social events. For example, going to the bar may not be something which the Asian colleague enjoys; indeed, alcohol may be prohibited to him on religious grounds.

So, there may be three issues:

● The white staff may have indicated through their behaviour that the Asian employee's presence was unwelcome.

- He may not enjoy the bar environment.
- The discussion of colleagues may revolve around things of no interest to him, for example drink.

Situation II
Feeling of relaxation and solidarity in own group; speaking own language. A not uncommon reaction by any given national or linguistic group, especially when the whole of the formal work is conducted in the majority language. It may be easier to communicate more freely in the first language, especially in social situations.

(b) What might be the perceptions of other staff?
Situation I

- He doesn't want to mix
- He's odd
- He's stand-offish.

Situation II

- When in Rome they should do as the Romans do
- They can't be bothered speaking English
- They are unfriendly and keep themselves to themselves
- They're talking about me/us (conspiratorially)
- They want to be on their own.

All the above assumptions, for Situations I and II, relate to assimilation, in other words 'they don't want to mix with us'; 'they are not fitting in with us.'

(c) What impact may this have on the minority ethnic employees in terms of career development and progression in the company?
This will depend upon the organisational culture. However, it is the informal networks which are at the heart of the management function and where the tricks of the trade are learnt. Also, the social aspect of work may be something in which staff are expected to participate. The social environment

may well be where informal networking goes on, for example where information about what is happening in the company is shared, people get to hear about job opportunities and useful contacts are made.

Situation I
The Asian man is likely to be excluded from this network, with negative consequences for his full participation in the organisation. This exclusion could reduce motivation, and result in low performance. This could lead to self-limiting behaviour, to the detriment of the organisation and himself.

Situation II
The African female staff may also be isolated from the mainstream informal networks, which are important for advancement within the organisation. This isolation may mean restricted access to management issues and decisions regarding policy.

Communication may take complicated forms if the group is perceived not to be fluent in the language of the majority, resulting in greater detriment to them. Such circumstances may produce rumour, distort information and increase the danger of misinterpreted messages circulating in the organisation.

(d) What impact may this have on the organisation?
These situations could mean that staff who experience exclusion may feel marginalised, devalued, demoralised or demotivated. This, in turn, could result in higher turnover of such employees. They may also not contribute to the organisation as fully as they could.

Situation I
The isolation might send out a message to other potential job applicants that this organisation would not be a comfortable environment for them. If this exclusion is typical, there will be a lack of role models for staff from many cultures, which may have an adverse impact on diversifying the pool of applicants from which recruitment could take place. This could, in turn,

hinder the development within the organisation of employees who are culturally different from those who have traditionally exercised managerial control and decision-making authority.

Situation II

The perception that different cultural groups don't mix in the organisation may develop and spill over from the social area into the workplace.

If people are then 'tiptoeing' around each other and not able to communicate in an open and relaxed way this may have an adverse impact on communication within the workplace, and therefore detract from the quality of the work itself.

However, if staff are grouping together from choice and there is a level of awareness of difference in the workforce and a welcoming of that diversity, this could reflect a positive environment, where everyone is welcomed on the basis of their ability to do the job and the contribution which they can make to the organisation. It would not be a problem that staff are not mixing socially because the atmosphere would be one where the choice was being freely made, and it would not be because of discomfort.

Checklist for action

- Speak to the staff from various cultural groups to find out why they don't mix more freely. Identifying the reasons will then help to address any problem. A more systematic way of obtaining staff feedback would be through a carefully prepared and administered attitude survey eliciting views on the state of cultural diversity in the organisation.
- Observe how workers are, individually or in groups, interacting with each other. If you notice that people are being marginalised or excluded, select one or two to discuss the issue and get a feel for why it is happening.
- Have lunch with a small group of colleagues; be sure to invite staff who reflect the range of cultures in the workforce.
- Organise social events which do not revolve exclusively

around activities associated with the dominant culture, for example going to the pub after work. The pub environment may exclude some minority groups either because they do not want to drink alcohol or because they feel uncomfortable in the pub environment. Instead, try to cater for a range of cultural interests, for example use of the coffee bar or arranging a sports event.

- Check the level of any communication difficulties. If there is a difficulty in mutual understanding, discuss that with colleagues of different cultural backgrounds and offer a solution, for example communication skills training.
- Address any issue of cultural or racial stereotyping through formal training events.

Peer pressure

Another barrier to change in the direction of cultural diversity which often emerges is peer pressure, or attributing the cultural antagonism to colleagues' attitudes rather than one's own. It might be summarised as: 'It's not me — I've nothing against them — but the team wouldn't like it'. This element of pressure from others is explored in the following two case studies.

Case study
Maintaining cultural homogeneity

A middle manager in a department which has been traditionally monocultural in the composition of its staff is asked about her recruitment practices. The manager says that she treats everyone the same. When pressed about why her team is, and always has been, culturally homogeneous, she says that *she* wouldn't mind a more culturally diverse workforce, but she would be concerned that such diversity might 'rock the boat'. The team is comfortable as it is at the moment and would find it difficult to accept anyone from outside their 'group'.

(a) What might really be the manager's situation?

The manager may be covering up her own hostile attitude by implying that the team will not accept diversification.

She may, however, have a genuine concern about the rest of her team, perhaps because of the environment which she has observed. The shift to a multicultural team would mean that she would have to address underlying issues which she might have been ignoring to date.

These underlying issues could relate to cultural antipathy, possibly expressed in the use of culturally offensive language, or unwritten practices conducive to the maintenance of the status quo. Job opportunities might be kept for people from that cultural group who already constitute the team, and might even be restricted, through pressure put on the manager, to family or friends of the current workforce.

Checklist for action

- Consider why you think diversifying the team would 'rock the boat'.
- If you think there is cultural antipathy within the team, identify what you base this belief on.
- Ensure that the images projected about the company – or your own team – include the widest possible range of cultural backgrounds. For example, include visual images of different cultures in your company literature. Have that literature displayed in your own office area. Ensure that there is no tolerance of racial or cultural insults, for example jokes which caricature, demean or are derogatory towards particular cultural groups and play on negative stereotypes.
- Review the recruitment process:

  —set selection criteria in accordance with the principle of the best person for the job
  —introduce recruitment panel interviews, with pre-shortlisting and pre-interview discussions regarding how to achieve the desired result
  —develop procedures to deal with harassment.

- Consider positive action in advertising for jobs.
- Openly discuss and debate negative views, stereotypes and valuations expressed about people belonging to cultures other than one's own.
- Encourage team members to explore any prejudicial views held.

Client pressure

The element of peer pressure can be extended to pressure from clients. Where, for example, does the individual manager or the organisation itself stand in policy terms if they are on the receiving end of client pressure when the client indicates that they do not want to be dealt with by a member (or members) of staff from a particular cultural background? Pressure on companies from clients to provide for cultural preferences is considered in the following case study.

Case study
Pressure on companies from clients to provide for cultural preferences

A consultancy firm offering services to a wide range of businesses has a team of five consultants. The team is mixed in terms of ethnic origin.

From time to time clients, who belong to a dominant cultural group, complain (as in any business). However, these complaints are predominantly about the consultants from other cultural backgrounds to themselves. The manager, at the request of the consultants, has investigated the complaints and she has found that she is being pressurised to supply the clients with consultants who share their backgrounds. This is not being expressed as overt discrimination, but the clients have 'expressed a preference' for the other consultants (who happen to fall into this category).

(a) What may be happening in this situation?
The following are possible:

- The consultants from other cultural backgrounds are underperforming
- There has been a lack of adequate feedback to these consultants
- They are being set up to fail
- Unclear objectives
- Inexplicit or higher expectations by the client of these consultants as opposed to their counterparts who belong to the culturally dominant group
- Lack of cooperation by the client towards the consultants from diverse cultural backgrounds
- Lack of resources allocated by the client to the consultancy project
- Clients are pressurising the supplier to discriminate.

(b) What may be the impact on the consultants who find themselves being singled out in this way?
The following are possible:

- There could be a lack of progress within the organisation
- They may lack exposure to a wide range of clients and therefore the loss of varied experience could lead to demotivation
- Lack of confidence in their own ability
- Less support from management
- Self-limiting behaviour
- Work experience gained is of less value.

(c) What may be the impact on the consultants from the culturally dominant group?

- They are pressurised to collude with racism
- They actually collude with this discrimination
- They have an increased workload, with a build-up of resentment because of that
- They feel superior
- A lessening of respect for consultants from other cultural backgrounds

- Greater confidence from feeling more valued by the client.

(d) What may be the impact on the organisation?

- Loss of client if they do not get the change of consultant
- Loss of other clients who may hear about the response
- Retention of client if consultant is changed

Checklist for action

Short-term

- When complaints are made by clients, speak immediately to the consultant concerned.
- Decide whether or not you and the consultant feel that this complaint relates to the race or culture of the consultant.
- Decide if the situation is really worth challenging.
- Decide what the goal is for the organisation.
- Evaluate whether or not the goal is achievable.
- Select the appropriate time and place to discuss with the client.

Long-term

- Ensure that all clients are aware of your company's stance on cultural diversity and its positive impact on quality – through your literature and all contracts drawn up with them.
- In initial training for all staff, particularly those who will have direct contact with clients, include discussion on issues associated with the principles of cultural diversity.
- Draw up guidelines for staff on how to deal with clients who indicate a preference for particular consultants on cultural or racial grounds. Include in their guidelines a briefing on equal opportunities so that staff are adequately prepared to pass this information to clients.
- Instruct consultants to report back to their supervisor or manager any incidents relating to racial prejudice so that staff can be supported if required.

- When possible, mix the teams and send two consultants together from different backgrounds to indicate to the client that a culturally or racially mixed team can operate effectively. This would be particularly useful at the beginning of a long contract.
- Ensure that the contract is clear, precise and the client's requirements are explicitly documented.

Exercise

Consider the following questions in relation to your own organisation or one with which you are familiar:

1. What would constitute positive action in the context of the organisation selected?
2. How would it be possible to introduce positive action?
3. What are the barriers to change in the selected organisation which may act against the development of a culturally diverse yet integrated team?
4. What could contribute to a removal of those barriers?

CHAPTER 3
The Benefits of the Diverse Team

Making it work – what's in it for the organisation?

The management of cultural diversity is more relevant to the business world today than it has ever been, but remains at the margin of the central concerns of businesses. This is partly because it is not generally seen as making a tangible contribution to the core objectives of the organisation.

Many organisations regard equal opportunities as a moral issue which is incompatible with the harsh realities of the market. However, the equality principle can also be a salient feature of business strategy. Institutions and companies are beginning to recognise the commercial damage they could suffer if they ignore the social concerns of the diverse communities in which they operate.

Importantly, the realisation is dawning that more and more consumers make choices based on their perception of the ethical positions of companies. Many consumers are no longer satisfied simply with the type of product or service provided. So an ethical edge in marketing is increasingly significant in business behaviour. A company can therefore enhance its profits and reputation by aligning itself with social responsibilities which appear to enhance the quality of life of the customer.

A major multinational UK food company, for example, is known for its policy of identifying suppliers, sub-contractors, staff and so on from a variety of cultural backgrounds. Many of their initiatives have taken into account the different communities among their consumers. This awareness has resulted in significant increases in their profit, not just from the increase in customers from the minority ethnic communities but also from others who feel positively about the company's values.

The globalisation of the market provides yet another reason for ethics to be woven into the fabric of business. It is increasingly less possible for companies to compete success-fully in other countries if they ignore the cultures and religions which are of importance for the consumers in those societies.

It is relevant from the business angle to note the changing population profile of the UK because of its implications for the changing nature of the customer base. The ability to work across cultures will be relevant to both managing the changing make-up of the organisation's external markets, and managing the increasingly diverse employee profile. Organisations are already coming to realise that unless traditional ways of thinking are set aside they are unlikely to survive. New ways of thinking are no longer a luxury but a necessity.

There is, for instance, no reason to stick to the assumption that homogeneous working groups are necessarily more productive and higher performing than heterogeneous ones. In fact, it can be argued that organisations employing 'clones', with similar experiences and training, those who 'fit the mould', are probably going to be less challenging and less likely to stimulate productive ideas to generate new solutions.

This is not to say that all homogeneous groups are inefficient or ineffective. However, what organisations have not been so convinced about in the past is that cultural diversity can also contribute positively to the competitiveness of the organisation by widening and enriching the pool of talented and skilled people. A range of 'different' people can help the organisation to become more flexible and adaptable to succeed in the fast-changing world.

Bringing ethics and business together is only part, though by no means an insignificant part, of the story. The other part is to do with the tangible, hard commercial and financial dimensions.

There is a growing recognition that even in the current poor economic climate skill shortages co-exist with high levels of unemployment and that, for talented people, it is still a seller's market. The impact on organisations lacking in skilled people is substantial. Compartmentalising, homogenising environments are unlikely to be hospitable to innovating, high-performing talents. Since the human resource is critical in gaining the competitive advantage, cultural diversity (combined with equality) provides a key ingredient in developing a motivating, empowering and energising atmosphere.

However, to attract talents out of the top drawer, an organisation needs to develop an external reputation based on its internal policies and initiatives as an employer that not only welcomes and values talent, but is sensitive to a diversity of needs.

On the other hand, if talents are ignored or mistreated there are real financial and other consequences. Discrimination lawsuits are becoming more expensive.

Much of the argument for cultural diversity and equal opportunities is common sense. If people feel unsupported or discriminated against their confidence will decline, and they are unlikely to perform at their best. If people are marginalised, or they feel that they have no other options, they are unlikely to show much enthusiasm in their activities. Moreover, untapped potential means an organisation under-utilising its human resources and failing to maximise the potential profitability of the company.

Motivation of others

Working towards cultural diversity in the workplace and effectively managing a diverse team implies that the goal is to have representation of a variety of cultures throughout the organisation, from the shopfloor to the boardroom. The number of opportunities available at the top of the organisation does not increase, so there will be more equal shares at all levels for all groups represented in society.

This realisation is often seen as a threat by the predominant group at the higher levels – mostly white, middle class, middle-aged men – because if the organisation is looking beyond the traditionally powerful group to recruit, beyond the talents available in the pool of white men, it follows that there will be more intense competition for a variety of opportunities.

Because of the sensitivity of promoting cultural diversity in the workplace, there are many barriers facing the manager who wants to develop an effectively performing team along these lines. It is important, therefore, to emphasise the benefits to the organisation, as this will motivate the workforce to be committed to the issue. It is vital to ensure that all members of staff – regardless of their cultural or ethnic origin, their age, their gender, etc – see how they might benefit from the development of diversity in the workplace.

An effective method of motivating managers and staff to incorporate diversity and equality into their mainstream work is to build objectives relating to this issue into the business plan of the organisation. This could be done by setting diversity targets. Departmental, team and individual objectives should then flow from the overall business objectives. Some ideas of how this has been done in organisations are:

Diversity targets

- Set overall diversity targets for the organisation.
- Make diversity part of managers' objectives, which they are then accountable for in appraisal, for example:
    —agreeing and working towards representation of staff from different cultural backgrounds in their team or department
    —attending a management of diversity training event
    —organising a diversity training programme for staff

> —building diversity objectives into staff members' individual workplans.
> - Monitor achievements against targets through managers' appraisals. Achievement of targets, or an account of innovative approaches to attempting to achieve targets, may then feed into incentive payments.

In order to motivate all sections of the organisation to work towards valuing diversity, the benefits need to be considered — personal, team, departmental, and organisational.

If it is possible to identify the benefits on all these levels this can motivate the workforce to use the skills of their current colleagues from different cultural backgrounds and improve the effectiveness of: the recruitment process; interaction in the team; performance within the team; progression within the organisation; customer care; expansion of the client base; and productivity.

Exercise
Consider the benefits of having a culturally diverse workforce. Can you identify what the benefits might be on a personal, departmental, and organisational level?

Personal	Departmental	Organisational

You may have included:

Personal	Departmental	Organisational
Widens managerial experience.	Maximises human resources available to the team.	Improves the wider public image of the organisation.
Develops a professional image.	Improves staff performance and motivation.	Eliminates unlawful discrimination, harassment or victimisation in the workplace (and helps avoid related expense of tribunal cases).
Increases mutual respect between colleagues.	Improves team working and motivation.	Enhances industrial relations within the company.
Satisfies own sense of fairness and justice.	Taps into a diverse range of talents for the work of the team.	Ensures that the organisation recruits and develops the best available people – by tapping into all sections of the community.
Develops own potential to the full.	Retains and develops diverse talents and skills.	Attracts into the company a wider range of staff with a broad range of skills.
Enhances communication skills.	Minimises the cost of recruitment, retention and training by reducing turnover and by selecting the right person for the job.	Increases the skills available to meet the needs of clients.
Opens up career prospects.		Enhances innovation and creative thinking, leading to problem-solving.
Increases individual motivation.		Enables effective management of rapid change.
		Brings the organisation closer to customer needs.
Able to work comfortably		Creates an environment where staff feel welcome.

Personal	Departmental	Organisational
and therefore at full potential.		If the organisation deals with cultural differences skilfully, those differences could be turned into a powerful advantage. Well-managed heterogeneous groups can outperform homogeneous groups in both quantity and quality – becoming more productive and profitable.
		Makes the organisation better able to deal with the changing demographics and the changing nature of the labour market which will contain more minority ethnic staff – and a greater mix both nationally and globally.
		Organisations become an 'employer of choice' – people positively choose the organisation from among many others.

The following four examples reflect the benefits of diversity to the business itself:

The business argument

Gaining the competitive edge

A branch of a high street recruitment agency, operating in an expanding new town with new businesses relocating there daily, found that they did not have a big enough range of job applicants available for their new clients. They were in danger of losing lucrative new business to a major competitor.

The manager had been aware for some time that a very limited number of the town's black residents were registered with them.

With the growth of their business the branch had recently expanded to try and cope and had employed a new recruitment consultant who happened to be black.

The impact of the new consultant just being in the office, visible to passers-by in the high street, was an immediate increase in black people calling in to enquire about job opportunities.

The branch has vastly increased its profitability.

Responding to differences

An engineering company has an equal opportunities policy and has had this in place for a number of years. An increasing number of staff from minority cultural backgrounds have been recruited into the company during the past few years and with this changing workforce the senior management team became conscious that the current practices and facilities might not be responding to the needs of the workforce. The senior management team decided to consult the workforce on a range of issues, including childcare, carer responsibilities, disability concerns and cultural issues. The findings were analysed and actions were agreed and prioritised. In relation to cultural issues, among those prioritised were:

(a) A racial harassment policy has been produced and a code of practice drawn up and communicated to the staff and managers.

(b) A wider range of dietary requirements are now catered for in the canteen, including the serving of halal meat once a week.

(c) A room has been set aside for the use of staff who wish to pray during the working day.

(d) Various versions of the uniform have been designed in order to reflect several different styles of dress; this has resulted in an increase of enquiries and subsequent applications for jobs from, in particular, Asian women.

(e) Flexibility with holiday arrangements has been introduced, so that staff wanting to take holidays at different times of the year for religious festivals can arrange their duties to do so.

The company has taken an active role in putting its equal opportunities policy into practice. Through the provision of a wider range of facilities and an open acknowledgement of the culturally diverse workforce, the company is creating an environment where staff learn about differences between cultures, and learn to appreciate and value those differences.

Rather than taking a 'colour blind' approach, where staff, regardless of their cultural or ethnic background, are expected to 'fit in' with the majority culture, the company is openly acknowledging the differing requirements of the staff and responding to these needs where possible.

Developing staff

A large public sector employer had a number of minority ethnic staff. However, they were only represented in the lower-grade jobs.

The management team did not want to highlight them by any form of positive action directed solely at them. Their concern was the possibility of a backlash from other staff. They consulted the lower-grade staff in order to identify their training needs and it emerged that there was a lot of frustration generally, because of the lack of opportunities for promotion.

This group of staff, which was predominantly minority ethnic people and white women, had a lot more that they could offer the organisation. For example, a number of the former were either graduates or had extensive experience from other organisations, but they were stuck at the junior support levels. Due to the strict hierarchical nature of the organisation, low-grade staff were not able to use their initiative and take on more responsibility, because that was stepping outside the boundaries of their job descriptions.

In consultation with the lower-grade staff, it was decided that a career development programme aimed at the needs of that group was required. The training and development programme was not designed to be solely for staff from minority cultural backgrounds − the issues which faced them in their work were the same as those of other staff. The equality issue was that the minority ethnic staff were disproportionately affected because they were represented at the lower levels in much greater numbers.

By consulting with the staff, the management were able to identify what could be done to break down the barriers facing this group. There were not yet any role models at senior levels for them in the organisation and this was contributing to a lack of confidence in the organisation that it would in fact be possible for them to progress to higher levels in this organisation.

The introduction of a career development programme for lower-grade staff contributed to building confidence among these staff in the organisation. Once some progress to more senior levels has been made, the organisation will have senior staff in place to act as role models for their current and future staff.

Keeping hold of the customer

A regional TV company estimated that by the end of the century a substantial proportion of their potential audience will comprise people from minority cultural backgrounds. Yet only a handful of their staff were from such backgrounds. Indeed, the percentage of applicants for journalists' posts was quite discouraging.

This difference in profile between their staff and their potential audience meant that they were in danger of losing touch with a substantial section of their audience, losing viewers and ultimately jeopardising their financial viability.

The company acted swiftly by making contacts in various cultural groups in its consumer area and targeting them with recruitment literature; introducing programmes dealing with a wider range of cultural issues; and encouraging relevant staff to take on more high-profile roles. All these initiatives have contributed to raising the profile of the company, promoting an image which is more attractive to the mixed community and more responsive to what its audience wants.

Senior managers also identify benefits to the company and its survival.

What the senior managers say ...

'We know that we can only succeed as a company if we have an environment that makes it easy for all of us, not just some of us, to work to our full potential.'

Senior manager, multinational pharmaceutical company

'We want to be the employer of choice. We want our pick of the talent out there.'

Senior manager, international computer company

'We need to develop more of a global vision to deal effectively in the international marketplace. The diversity encouraged in the workplace will help us build that global perspective.'

Senior manager, multinational food group

And the employees reflect their views on the benefits of diversity.

What employees say ...

'When I graduated with a degree in business studies I was interested in applying for work in the financial sector. I selected which companies to apply to on the basis of whether or not they had an equal opportunities policy because I feel that I stand a greater chance of progressing to senior management in a company which says it is committed to equal opportunities.'

(Jewish female)

'I was particularly attracted to apply to this retail company because they indicated in the company literature that the uniform was flexible to allow Asian women to wear traditional dress. I was not interested in applying to companies who didn't make this clear at the outset. There is the additional facility of a prayer room.'

(Asian Muslim female)

'I have found in my work, which involves counselling people who have extreme financial difficulties, that I can work equally well with black and white clients – both men and women. However, I know that the fact that I am black has made it easier for some of my clients to speak more openly with me. Sometimes white colleagues have asked me to help them advise black clients. They don't always need to do this, but just on occasions they have found it helpful to be able to call in a black colleague. I don't mind – that's what team work is about.'

(Black male)

Exercise

Consider the following in relation to your own team or organisation, or one with which you are familiar:

1. What benefits do you think there are for the organisation if it has a culturally diverse workforce?

2. Could more be gained from the situation? If so, how do you think that could happen?

CHAPTER 4

Management Dilemmas in the Culturally Diverse Team

Managing a culturally diverse team requires positive commitment. It demands that managers apply policies and practices developed under the heading of 'equal opportunities' but requires them to recognise limitations inherent in approaching the issue of diversity in this way.

A well-implemented diversity policy and programme of action should result in equality of access to the employment and career development opportunities in the organisation. With the greater access there should be a change in the staff profile – in particular in relation to gender, race, disability and any other issues which the organisation has incorporated within its diversity policy.

Having tapped the potential of a wider range of people, the manager now has the opportunity to use the new range of skills available. However, as many people have relatively little experience of working with colleagues from different cultural backgrounds, a number of new situations may arise with which managers have not been trained to deal, or which may be outside their previous experience. If consideration is to be given to improving the situation for people from minority cultures in the workplace, the role of managers and the impact of their attitudes and behaviour on staff could be particularly significant.

The issues which can arise and which are explored below are:

- The emergence of segregated groups in the workplace
- Utilising the skills of staff from diverse cultural backgrounds
- Access to development opportunities
- Giving appropriate feedback to culturally diverse staff
- Cross-cultural communication skills for all staff
- Support networks for individual staff members from specific cultural or ethnic groups.

There needs to be an awareness of differences, including different experiences and customs, in order to operate effectively in a culturally diverse team.

This chapter poses a number of dilemmas which face the manager of a culturally diverse workforce and offers ideas on dealing with them.

The following case study focuses on how minority groups can become isolated from the mainstream of the organisation. Ideas are offered as to how such situations might be managed.

Case study
Managing uneasy relationships

An organisation in the public sector has a large proportion of Asian men, age range 35–50, who are represented in the lower-grade, skilled jobs. A shift system operates. Over the years the white workers have formed teams and the Asian workers have formed teams, each group working different shift patterns. The management have found it more convenient to organise the shifts mostly on these ethnic grounds.

However, in recognition of the radically changed nature of the working environment and the transformation it has wrought in the perceptions of the workforce with regard to relations and processes, the management team decide to introduce a diversity policy. In initial discussions, one of the managers raises his concern that Asian male staff in the company have always been addressed formally, ie as Mr, but that the other men have always been addressed by their first names. This makes him uncomfortable and he also feels that this practice is contributing to the divisions in the workforce.

His dilemma is that he is unsure whether to open up the discussion or just to leave things as they are. He decides to tackle the issue. Having developed the confidence to broach this subject with the Asian staff, he discovers that this situation has developed because the rest of the staff could not pronounce the Asian men's first names. The Asian staff either accepted being addressed by their surnames, because it was easier and less embarrassing, and they then became known by them; adapted their name to an 'English sounding' name; or they were given nick-names which were easily pronounced by other colleagues.

(a) Why has the manager not addressed the issue of culturally segregated shifts before now?
The key issues for management are the smooth, efficient and productive running of the operation. For this to happen it needs to exercise control and it must ensure as little disruption of production as possible through harmonious industrial relations. Thus the management might have felt that it could maximise these features through segregated shifts. The reasons for this policy might be as follows:

- There is an assumption that cultural diversity hinders group performance.
- There is an assumption that it is easier for culturally homogeneous groups to establish harmonious relations necessary for the smooth working of the operations.
- The white staff are not prepared to work in a shift where they are in a minority.
- The white staff are not prepared to work with minority cultures because of cultural antipathy.
- The management have perceived their exercise of control over culturally homogeneous shifts is easier and communication is more efficiently handled.

One of the main factors which affects the manager initially in communicating effectively with the Asian workers is lack of confidence. This can result in uneasiness when managing Asian staff, particularly when they form part of a mixed team. All of which feeds into fear or disempowerment which can result in the manager being immobilised.

(b) What might be the impact of 'treating people differently' in this way?
This immobilisation can result in the Asian staff being ignored, with the result that they are not asked to contribute to the organisation in the same way as the rest of the staff, for example by taking on areas of responsibility, and this then affects their progression in the company.

This is a common experience for staff from minority cultural backgrounds. The different initial treatment in practice then becomes a more formal working relationship with them, especially when compared with the manager's relationship with the white staff.

When managers address the two groups differently, there is a highlighting of 'them' and 'us'. The Asian workers may feel devalued as, in this organisation, a formal mode of address if used for subordinates indicates a lack of familiarity. It can also suggest distancing, which may become an obstacle to teamworking.

And of course they do 'like' to keep themselves to themselves, if their treatment in the other group is such that they are differentiated from the majority, and the relationship is uneasy. The impact on the organisation can be lower productivity, if, for example, different shifts of workers do not communicate effectively when they are handing over from one shift to another. This lack of mixing can also project a poor image to the external world, including clients and prospective employees.

Checklist for action

● Begin by asking one or two of the Asian staff how they

would like to be addressed. State your own discomfort at addressing them differently from the other staff.

- Familiarise yourself with one or two first names, writing them down both as they are spelt and also as they are pronounced, so that you can remember them more easily.
- Use the names when speaking to other members of staff so that others become more familiar with them. Correct others if the wrong pronunciation of colleagues' names is being used.
- As appropriate, ensure that first names are on any name badges, notices, doors or correspondence with staff.

A danger of which managers of a culturally diverse team must be aware and seek to counter is the problem of the organisation marginalising minority staff and failing to use them effectively in the team. The following case study explores this problem.

Case study
Making the best use of minority ethnic staff

**'The minority ethnic workers will be able to
respond to the needs of our minority ethnic clients.'**

On the face of it, the above statement links directly to the need to develop a diverse workforce in order to meet the needs of clients more effectively. However, there are dangers of taking such a simplistic approach to the benefits of a diverse workforce.

A care assistant of Chinese origin has recently been appointed to a job in a residential home for the elderly in an area where there is quite a culturally mixed client population. Before the new employee arrived, the staff in the home were all of UK origin. The elderly people are mostly of UK origin, although recently a few people belonging to other cultures have moved in.

The manager is delighted that the new care assistant is a Chinese woman, as three of the new residents are of Chinese origin and there have been some difficulties for staff in communicating with them.

At first, the new assistant is happy to be able to contribute to the residential home with her special expertise as a bilingual worker. However, after a few months it is apparent to her that:

- She is being used as an interpreter, but has not had the appropriate training, nor does she have the required professional support (and she also doubts her own ability as a professional interpreter).
- Her work as an interpreter is not being recognised; she still has her full-time job to do, and her workload is much heavier than that of the other staff because of the time spent interpreting for visiting professionals.
- Her own professional development is suffering because she is not getting the wider experience in her job that she should be doing.
- She is spending all of her time caring and interpreting for particular clients and not developing her expertise in responding to the needs of the clients as a whole.

(a) How might this member of staff feel in the situation?

- This member of staff does not want to be seen as unwilling to do what is required. She may also feel that it is important for someone to help these clients.
- She may feel stressed in the job because of the responsibility over and above her role.

(b) What are the management issues arising?

- Concern about the standard of interpreting when an unqualified interpreter is being used, particularly to interpret for other professionals whose field the interpreter may not be familiar with.
- Chinese worker's workload – stress may build up because of the extra demands on this person's time.
- The manager may be working on the basis that staff will

make complaints if they have too much work. This will not necessarily be true in all cultures.

- Chinese worker's experience in all areas of the job — she is not being allowed the time to develop in all areas of the work and may therefore not develop the skills to care for the white elderly residents.
- Development of other staff's skills to care for the minority ethnic elderly. Other staff may become dependent on the Chinese worker to care for the Chinese elderly. This means that they are not effectively working within the multi-cultural community.
- Segregation — this situation could encourage 'white looking after white, Chinese looking after Chinese', at the expense of multi-skilling the workforce. This segregation may not provide a high quality of service to the clients.
- The non-English speaking clients have to communicate through an interpreter. Consequently, the relationship between the specialist or doctor and the client can be adversely affected because the specialist cannot communicate directly with the client. This is of particular concern when information of an intimate or personal nature is to be relayed, or if important or distressing information is requested or given.
- In a residential home providing a service to a culturally diverse community, more attention should be paid to having a culturally diverse workforce, so that the skills are available from more than one staff member. This would serve the purpose of relieving the pressure on one staff member and of offering more choice to the clients.

Checklist for action

- Consult the Chinese worker to see if she wants to continue acting as an interpreter. If so, then appropriate professional training should be provided.
- Introduce the payment of a language allowance for staff whose linguistic skills are being used for either interpreting or translating.

- Staff who speak English only should be provided with training in how to communicate effectively through an interpreter.

Communication within an organisation is vital to effective management. Managers with responsibility for a culturally diverse team may experience difficulty in actually communicating with some of their workforce. The following case study focuses on the difficult but important task of giving feedback to staff from minority ethnic backgrounds.

Case study
Giving feedback to minority ethnic staff

A project team is carrying out work which involves a high level of commitment to the task and requires all members to contribute effectively in order to meet the stipulations of the contract with the client. There is one minority ethnic person in the team and he is performing poorly.

The project manager identifies a low level of skill in this worker in one particular area. However, as the other team members are 'bending over backwards' and it has not affected meeting the clients' deadlines, the manager avoids pointing out the gaps to him.

Over the course of the project, the minority ethnic member of the team begins to notice that he is being given the least important and more routine tasks. Eventually he complains to the project manager about the allocation of tasks. His complaint is that he is not being allocated tasks appropriate to his qualifications and experience, and that this is a form of indirect racial discrimination because it will affect his performance in the job and ultimately his prospects for promotion.

The project manager is completely at a loss as to how to handle the situation, which reaches a stalemate, until the performance of the team is affected and the project manager is called to account for this to senior management.

(a) What reactions might a project manager from the majority culture have?
A variety of emotions and reactions is possible:

- Fear of being perceived as racist and accused of being racist by the minority ethnic staff member
- Fear that the accusation of racism may result in an industrial tribunal case
- Fear that his or her own prejudices may indeed be having an effect on team interaction and are leading to different treatment of the minority ethnic worker
- Insecurity about communicating with minority ethnic staff.

(b) What reactions might a minority ethnic project manager have?
The manager's emotions and reactions may include:

- Lack of confidence as a result of feeling vulnerable within the company
- Fear of being perceived as not demonstrating solidarity, and of acting against 'own people'
- Fear of accusation of colluding with the management in racism
- Concern that if they do not give appropriate feedback then the minority ethnic staff member will continue to perform badly, and this may reflect on the manager.

(c) What management issues arise in this situation?

- The need for an awareness of discrimination and dis-advantage in society, and the possibility that this then reproduces itself in the workplace.
- The need for knowledge about the organisation's equal opportunities policy and codes of practice. The awareness that the policy is aimed at maximising the potential of all members of staff, and that this involves access to development opportunities and appropriate feedback when staff are under-performing, for example through staff appraisals.

- Cross-cultural communication skills, which are then applied to:
  —team building
  —coaching/mentoring
  —motivating
  —listening
  —dealing with confrontation
  —risk-taking.

Checklist for action

- Consider whether you give feedback equally to all members of staff, regardless of their cultural or racial background.
- Give immediate feedback to the minority ethnic member of the team, with a clear indication of the area where they are lacking in adequate skills which the job requires.
- Offer a range of remedies, including training, suggested reading and opportunities to develop skills on specific named projects.
- Build into each project plan feedback on performance for each individual member of the team.
- Encourage team members to identify their own short-comings or needs as soon as they become apparent, rather than when it is too late to remedy them.

The above case study concentrates on the ineffective communication skills of the manager. The other element to consider is the ability of the minority ethnic employees to communicate effectively with staff from different cultural backgrounds to their own.

The following case study explores the need for effective communication skills.

Case study
Cultural diversity and staff appraisal

A senior, long-serving Asian male manager of a research and development section in a pharmaceuticals company, internationally renowned in his field, is concerned that he is never asked to take overall responsibility for the organisation in the absence of the managing director when he is away on business. Other managers, with less experience than him, are routinely asked to take on this task.

The Asian manager is the only one who is passed over in this way. He decides that, as his annual appraisal is coming up, he will raise this issue with the managing director at that meeting.

When the subject is raised, the managing director looks uncomfortable and says that the manager is highly competent on the technical side, but lacks the communication skills and leadership qualities required to do the job and to deal effectively with the staff and clients in a generalist management role. The Asian manager replies that he has not been given the chance to demonstrate his ability. Neither has he had any indication of his need to develop these skills. Performance of staff in his department is very high and he has never had complaints about his management style.

(a) Identify what may be going wrong and why

- It is not clear what criteria are being used to assess effective communication skills and leadership style. Therefore the manager has nothing to measure his performance against.
- The manager has had no ongoing feedback, indicating where he might be underperforming. If there is a skills gap, he has had no encouragement to acquire those skills through training or development opportunities.

(b) What is the possible impact on the individual, the team, other minority staff in the organisation, the organisation?

- The individual:
  —demotivation
  —feeling of resentment
  —withdraw into themselves
  —lack of cooperation with the managing director

—may look for another job.
- The team:
  —lose cooperation of team members
  —lose contribution/guidance of experienced members of the team.
- Other minority staff:
  —demotivation
  —anger
  —implication that they too will not have a chance to progress
  —reinforces negative view of the organisation.
- The organisation:
  —shows lack of confidence in ethnic minority staff – which may then have an effect on how white staff work with them
  —loss of maximum return on the investment they have made over a long period
  —loss of contribution from experienced manager
  —may affect recruitment
  —poor image internally and externally.

Checklist for action

- Acknowledge potential for differential treatment of individual staff members who are a minority within a culturally diverse group.
- Ensure that assessment criteria are appropriate for staff from a variety of cultural backgrounds.
- Communicate the assessment criteria to all staff.
- Monitor the application of assessment criteria in the appraisal process.
- Check for a fair distribution of development opportunities.

Case study
Pitfalls in cross-cultural communication

An organisation has a representative number of minority ethnic staff, some of whom have progressed to middle-management level. It finds that, although the staff from majority and minority cultural backgrounds interact formally (as reflected in the organisational structure), there have been misunderstandings between them.

The minority ethnic staff are perceived to be aggressive in their style of communication. This has included speaking loudly, sometimes shouting; appearing to dominate discussions through taking up a lot of time in meetings; withdrawing from discussions in an abrupt way; and sitting apart from the rest of the group in meetings. Several other staff have indicated, informally, and not directly to their minority ethnic colleagues, that they feel intimidated by some of them and therefore there is a lack of collaboration in work.

The result of this situation, which is not spoken about openly, is that staff are hesitant in each other's company, the few senior minority members of staff are isolated from their peers, and this in turn affects their performance.

(a) What might be at play in this interaction?
The situation may be new for all concerned. In the past, minority ethnic staff have been in the lower-grade jobs and there is therefore little shared experience on either side of working in a culturally mixed team at management level. Although current relationships are in theory between equals, past experience is preventing effective communication between the two parties. There may be an attempt to impede their full participation and thus 'engineer' their failure. It may be that minority ethnic managers are not being heard.

(b) What might be the perception of majority staff?
The perception may be that minority ethnic staff have a different communication style which appears to be either aggressive or generally not in tune with the communication style of the organisation. Experience shows that avoidance tactics may be used, which will result in the minority ethnic staff not getting exposure to the range of experience which they should.

Some feel insecure with their minority ethnic colleagues,

intimidated by them, and shy away from contact with them. This is bound to have an adverse affect on their working relationships.

(c) What might be the perception of minority ethnic staff?
'Aggression' may be perceived as appropriate behaviour which leads to progression in an organisation. However, while this behaviour from a white manager may be considered to be 'go-getting' and evaluated positively, from a minority manager it is perceived as 'aggressive', 'getting above their station' and therefore evaluated negatively. This is similar to the different evaluation of the behaviour of women managers as opposed to their male counterparts.

The perception of minority ethnic staff could be that they must demonstrate their abilities that much more than other staff have to, just to get the same recognition and to get to the same level in the organisation. Again, a parallel here could be drawn with the experiences of women, who often find that they have to 'prove themselves' much more than male colleagues.

The perception of the minority ethnic staff could also be that the other staff feel awkward with them, but that they get no clear message why there is this awkwardness — differences are skirted around rather than addressed openly.

Checklist for action

- Make sure that staff of all cultural and racial backgrounds have effective communication skills or have the opportunity to acquire them.
- Consider offering training to address the specific inter-personal and communication skills needs of minority ethnic staff.
- Be particularly alert to staff interactions in a team if one of the team is the only person in a minority because of their culture or race, and look out for signs of exclusion or avoidance.
- Support minority ethnic managers in their decisions,

particularly if they are new in the post. Use supportive words and body language, encouraging participation in meetings and giving positive feedback in front of others.

A cultural diversity policy can only be effective when it has the support of the management behind it, but some organisations may fail to recognise the extent to which their own culture is influenced by the dominant culture outside it. Making a cultural diversity policy work in some circumstances can be a challenging prospect. To be successful, the manager needs to address the issue of organisational culture.

Case study
Managing diversity within a traditional, exclusive culture

A public sector institution has a well-publicised equal opportunities policy, with clear guidelines on the whole recruitment and selection process, from identifying the vacancy through to job design, interviewing and decision-making.

However, career progression is in fact heavily dependent upon getting into the 'in-group', that informal network which exists in many organisations. Once in the network, information about how to progress is gathered in a variety of informal settings inside and outside the workplace. Whether or not this is openly acknowledged, the effect is that there can be antipathy towards people perceived to be outsiders. Social and informal facilities are designed mainly to meet traditional white male needs. Leisure activities are orientated to that group – the centre of informal social activity is often the bar, which presents an image of a macho and alcohol-related culture – alienating and isolating for those who do not wish to participate in it.

The result in this organisation is that the promotion rate of minority ethnic staff is much lower than that of other staff. Women would be equally excluded if this kind of system were in operation.

(a) Can you guess what the cultural composition of the above workforce is?
It is unlikely that there will be many minority ethnic staff. In this case the minority ethnic staff feel 'alienated and isolated' — this is not usual if there are large numbers in an organisation.

(b) What factors might be operating against minority ethnic staff in terms of progression in the organisational hierarchy?
Lack of access to the kind of information about potential job opportunities; developmental opportunities by working on special projects etc, which is passed around at these informal gatherings. Lack of encouragement from senior levels.

The minority ethnic staff are not part of the informal network in the organisation. This should not be under-estimated; in this organisation they are excluded from these social events and opportunities to network informally, and this has an adverse impact on their progress.

Checklist for action

- Consult all staff to check that any facilities provided by the organisation do in fact cater for their needs.
- Consider setting up a mentoring system (see page 103), aimed at ensuring that minority ethnic staff in particular have someone in the organisation who can 'show them the ropes' and ensure their inclusion in key discussions — formal and informal. This mentoring system could form part of staff induction.
- Ensure that social activities do not revolve exclusively around alcohol-related events.
- Provide a range of foods from different cultures both at social events and in the canteen.
- Encourage discussion about cultural differences rather than concentrate on the majority — for example, different foods, family structure, religion.

The following initiative is a positive measure which gives a feeling of exclusion to the majority and may not lead to a collaborative atmosphere in the organisation if it is ineffectively managed.

Case study
Dealing with resentment towards a black workers' group

Over a period of about five years Sally, who is a manager within a private sector organisation, has seen her team change in cultural composition. From what was a white team staffed predominantly by white staff, the team now includes 4 black staff out of a total of 15 people.

The black staff participate in team meetings, but they are not heard equally. For example, on a number of occasions their suggestions have been ignored.

A few incidents have occurred; some 'lighthearted' jokes have been made to one of the black staff about what they have brought in for their lunch and comments about the smell of the food have been made; some language used by white colleagues has been subtly, and sometimes not so subtly, objected to by black staff. The use of the term 'coloured' about clients raised the black staff's objection that the term 'coloured' was imposed on them in the past defining them in a subordinate and oppressive relationship, and black people have now adopted the term 'black', asserting the element of choice born of independent status. The white staff's view is that the black staff were being 'over-sensitive' and that the objections which they have made to the use of language should not be taken seriously. The behaviour of the white staff remained unchanged.

Two black members of staff approached the manager and asked if a black workers' group could be set up. This would involve the black staff in a meeting over a lunch period once a month, using one of the seminar rooms available on the company premises. The manager agreed, allocating a modest budget to the group for photocopying in order to distribute information and papers for the meetings, and to provide a sandwich lunch.

This resulted in murmurings among white staff that a white workers' group should be set up. A delegation of white workers went to Sally to request this. Their request was denied on the grounds that their needs were already being catered for and the request, emanating from feelings of resentment towards the black workers, was unjustified.

(a) In your view, what were the needs of the black workers and why did they request support for a black workers' group?
The black workers may have felt the need for the following:

- To develop and exchange ideas on strategies to cope with their working environment, where they are made to feel they are in a cultural minority, resulting in feelings of disempowerment.
- To secure an appropriate, safe, dedicated forum to discuss experiences as black workers in a predominantly white, and sometimes hostile, working environment.
- To empower the group to participate more effectively in the organisation – for example to be listened to in team meetings.
- To relax and develop solidarity with colleagues who all have some common experiences of racial discrimination in a predominantly white working environment.

(b) What was the intention of the manager in supporting this group?
From the action of the manager, the intention appears to be:

- To support the black workers through the provision of a forum in which they can meet.
- To send a signal to the white workers that black workers have particular needs and that those needs would be supported by the organisation, thus establishing a sense of fairness among all staff.
- Possibly to be perceived as not being racist (by black staff and by white staff).

(c) What may have been behind the reactions of the white staff?
The white staff are showing that they resent the black staff

coming in to the team and not 'fitting in'. They appear neither to have experience of working with colleagues of different ethnic origins nor to recognise the needs of black colleagues.

(d) What other possible consequences are there for inter-relations between black and white workers in the organisation?
This initiative may seem to address the symptoms rather than the cause of the tension between black and white workers, which appear to lie in the attitudes and behaviour of the latter group. Thus this action may do little to improve the quality of communication within the organisation. Indeed, it may worsen as the two groups segregate and polarise.

Checklist for action

- Feedback is needed from the white workers to establish why they continue to interact with their black colleagues in antagonistic ways. Once their reasons have been identified, it may be possible to formulate strategies such as a range of training, together with the formation of the black workers' group, that would enhance understanding, and impact on counterproductive attitudes and dysfunctional behaviour.
- Ensure that all staff understand the concept of positive action (see page 48) and are aware that it is part of the organisation's policy. This information should be provided through:
  —a company bulletin
  —newsletters
  —memos
  —briefing meetings
  —training sessions.
- Encourage staff to challenge discriminatory remarks or actions through the following guidelines:
  —do not attack the statement or behaviour, but question the underlying assumptions
  —do not attack the person, but offer information on the impact or the possible impact of the statement or behaviour

—show respect to the other person
—offer/encourage solutions.
- Offer training to all staff. This training should include developing effective challenging skills, particularly on how to challenge racist or offensive comments and behaviour. This training might include consideration of:
  —the values and assumptions underlying the behaviour of the person being challenged
  —the response of the individual who wants to challenge and how that challenge is made
  —the long-term organisational strategy towards a more enduring solution to the issues.
- Develop ownership through the following:

Policy
—Consult with staff while developing the written policy or statement.
—Produce the policy or statement to a high standard, giving it importance within the context of the other organisational policies.
—Demonstrate commitment through high-profile senior management communication about the policy/statement; this should be in written and spoken form, and demonstrated through the behaviour of senior management − by example from the top.
—Keep staff up to date with changes in the policy as it is amended and developed.

Communication
—Circulate the policy or statement to all departments.
—Exhibit the policy or statement on all display boards.
—Include items on cultural diversity in the standard company newsletter, bulletin, or in special communications from the chief executive or senior manager.
—Design quality poster displays.
—Hold roadshows and exhibitions on cultural diversity − particularly at the launch of the new policy.

Structure

—Invest power and authority in either an individual with responsibility for cultural diversity, or in a group such as a cultural diversity committee or working group.
—Identify people who can act as advisers in specific areas, such as racial discrimination, or racial harassment.
—Carry out publicity and promotion of these specialist advisers and their areas of expertise.
—Ensure that advisers are equipped to brief individual departments on policy development and its implementation.

Training

—Introduce training for all staff. Sessions should be introduced by a senior manager to demonstrate the high level of commitment given to the issue by the senior management team.
—Carry out targeted training for specific groups of staff (eg on recruitment and selection, cross-cultural communication skills and development skills for lower-grade staff).

Part of the responsibility of taking any kind of positive action is to ensure that the workforce understands what positive action is in terms of the law. They should understand why it is an important element of a cultural diversity policy, and they should also know and appreciate what the organisation's policy is in relation to it. Furthermore, they need to understand why the action is taking place, what their individual responsibilities are and what part they should be playing in implementing and supporting such policies.

Exercise

1. What issues in your experience have arisen in a culturally diverse workforce?
2. What issues do you envisage may arise in working in a

culturally diverse workforce in relation to:

- Recruitment?
- Staff training and development?
- Teamwork?

3. How could these issues be addressed, with positive outcomes for the staff, the management and the clients of the organisation?

CHAPTER 5
Achieving Results

So far we have looked at the issues which relate to cultural diversity in the workplace – the principles, the barriers, the benefits and the operational dilemmas which may arise. We now consider ways in which we can make things happen and translate the theory into practice – at organisational, team and individual levels.

Organisational action

In order to maximise the potential of all staff, particularly in a culturally diverse workforce, a strong lead needs to come from the top. How can a positive attitude to working in a diverse group be developed in an organisation? What action can be taken to ensure that the environment is conducive to a high level of performance from the whole of the workforce? Action is considered from the point of view of the organisation and of the individual manager.

If managers are motivated to ensure the best use of the human resources available, they will probably want to develop the skills required to manage the team and invest the required resources into planning the utilisation of the whole of the workforce more effectively. However, the development of individual managers is limited by the organisational framework and policies within which they operate.

The following examples indicate action which can be taken by the organisation.

Ethnic monitoring

What use are statistics; how well are you doing as an organisation or team? What indicators does an organisation use to decide how well the organisation is attracting and retaining the best staff from as wide a pool as possible?

Employers are encouraged by legislation to identify potential areas of direct and indirect discrimination against specific groups and, if cultural under-representation is identified, to take positive action to correct the imbalance. A guide to identifying under-representation is to consider the ethnic composition of the community in the geographical location from which the organisation usually recruits. The ethnic composition of the workforce should then be compared with the community representation.

Equality monitoring, and the collection of information on ethnic origin from applicants for jobs and for promotion once in the organisation, can provide the necessary data to identify potential areas of under-representation, and possible direct or indirect discrimination. The procedure is similar to many long-established ways in which management monitor other aspects of their business, such as costs, cash-flow, progress against budgets and plans, sickness absences and labour turnover. This monitoring data is then used by managers to review their progress and to identify areas which may require particular attention.

The first step in ethnic monitoring is to collect information about the ethnic composition of the current workforce, and to keep that system up to date by adding the details of new staff and deleting the information about leavers. Technically, this should be a straightforward process, similar to the process used for the collection and study of many items of personal data which go through the personnel record system.

However, there is often resistance to the collection of information about staff's ethnic origin. Senior managers need to be aware of the potential for this resistance, as it may result in a low response rate, which will then affect the usefulness of the data collected. The resistance is often based upon misunderstandings.

The majority ethnic staff perceive that the data will be used to give 'preferential treatment' to minority staff, whereas the minority staff fear that the data will be used to 'de-select' them from opportunities. Both these reactions indicate a lack of understanding of equality principles and practices.

Information should be given to staff before the monitoring exercise begins so they understand the purpose for which the data is being collected. It can increase the response rate if the request goes out under the signature of the most senior member of the management team. Of course, the first step which the senior management team should take is to clarify their own understanding of why they are collecting the data.

Once collected, it is vital that the data is collated, analysed and a summary communicated to the workforce, along with information about how the data is going to be used. If under-representation is identified, this may alter recruitment planning. If minority staff are grouped in specific departments, the reasons for this should be investigated.

However, experiences in some organisations show that a lack of preparation of the workforce will affect the response rate. Some organisations have experienced one or more of the following:

- Low response rate
- Return of destroyed forms
- Return of intentionally incorrect data.

Some of the issues which arise in introducing an ethnic monitoring system are explored in the following case study.

Case study
Introducing ethnic monitoring in an organisation

A company decides to address the fact that it is not a culturally diverse organisation. It is very monocultural in its employee profile, and has a staff mix which does not reflect the population in its catchment area. The company's customer base reflects the staff mix. The management team wishes to attract customers from the whole of the community and recognises that this is unlikely to be achieved without developing a culturally diverse workforce.

In order to plan the recruitment process, the management decide to collect data regarding the ethnic origin of the current staff. An ethnic monitoring form was designed and circulated to all staff.

The initial response rate was low, and a number of people returned their forms with comments to the effect that they were not going to give information about their ethnic origin.

(a) What is the purpose of collecting the data?
The management took this action to get information about minority representation in the organisation. They wanted to evaluate to what extent the workforce reflected the local population. They would then be in a position to set an achievable target for the organisation to meet. This information is required so that they can plan the allocation of resources required to address the issue of under-representation.

(b) Why might staff not have cooperated?
Staff may have reacted in this way due to lack of understanding of the relevance and usefulness of data on cultural diversity within the organisation. The perception may be that everyone is, or should be, treated the same, and that people should not be identified by their ethnic origin.

There may also be a suspicion that this data is being gathered to give preferential treatment, in terms of jobs and promotion prospects, to particular groups. The impact of this could be a backlash from the current staff. There could also be anxiety about what use might be made of the information in the future.

(c) At what stages should monitoring be carried out in an organisation?
Suggested stages, information required, possible findings and ideas for action are itemised in the following chart.

Stage	Information required	Possible findings	Ideas for action
Organisational	How many of each ethnic origin category are currently employed in each job and grade?	Under-representation of particular categories of staff throughout the organisation or under-representation at senior levels, with areas of over-representation lower down or in particular sections or functions.	Positive action in advertising campaigns; staff development programmes for minority ethnic and/or lower-grade staff; introduction of mentoring programme.
Recruitment	How many of each ethnic origin category apply for entry to the organisation? To what jobs and grades? What are the success rates?	Low level of applications to the organisation. High level of applications to the organisation, but low success rate.	If low level of applications – positive action in advertising. If high level of applications but low success rate – investigate recruitment process for equal opportunities, including practices of recruiters.
Promotion	How many of each ethnic origin category apply for promotion within the organisation? What are the success rates?	Low level of applications for promotion. High level of applications for promotion, but low success rate.	If low level of applications for promotion – actively encourage minority ethnic staff to apply for promotion. If high level of applications for promotion – investigate promotion process for equal opportunities, including practices of appraisers and promotion board or decision-makers.

Stage	Information required	Possible findings	Ideas for action
Qualifications	What relevant qualifications are held by these categories in each job and grade?	Higher qualifications held by individuals from minority ethnic backgrounds than for their white counterparts at the same level of job in the organisation.	Investigate access to promotion opportunities.
Length of service	How long have people in each ethnic origin category spent in each grade?	Minority ethnic staff taking longer to gain promotion and move up in the hierarchy.	Investigate reasons for not progressing in the promotion process, and also investigate reasons for not coming forward.
Wastage	How many of each ethnic origin category leave the organisation? For what reasons?	Minority ethnic staff leaving either more quickly or for reasons which relate to lack of development opportunities and promotion. Another possible reason for leaving could be related to the environment – racism and racial harassment.	Put in place, or investigate, current exit interview procedure. Focus groups with minority ethnic staff to check reasons for high turnover.
Education and training	How many of each ethnic origin category attend training courses at the organisation's expense?	Minority ethnic staff not receiving training funded by the organisation at the same level or rate as white staff.	Investigate information given out about funded training opportunities.

Grievance and disciplinary	How many complaints are brought by each ethnic origin category of staff? What are the complaints in relation to?	Different level of complaints from minority ethnic staff. Could be higher, indicating poorer environment than for white staff. Could be lower, which may indicate lack of confidence in coming forward.	Monitor types of complaint. Communicate effectively the grievance procedure to all staff. Take action on grievances brought.
Harassment	How are instances of harassment identified and monitored?	No consistent approach to monitoring racial harassment as distinct from other forms of complaint.	Develop, communicate and implement a policy on racial harassment. Monitor complaints. Set up advisers on harassment.
Pay and other terms and conditions of employment	What salaries are earned by workers in each job and grade? What about access to overtime? What about fringe benefits?	Lower average income for minority ethnic staff as compared with white counterparts at similar levels.	Investigate system of pay and remuneration for equal opportunities.

(d) What benefits do you think there are in introducing ethnic monitoring into an organisation?
A number of benefits as a result of ethnic monitoring have been identified by a variety of organisations:

- It forms part of effective human resource management – being able to respond to requests for information and being able to defend the organisation against complaints.
- It is a management tool which makes managers formally aware of what is happening in their departments and enables them to question practices.
- The organisation is seen to be a fair employer – which is important for current and potential employees.
- It enhances the public image of the organisation.
- It offers fair selection and the best people are appointed.
- It forms part of good business and employment practice.
- It complies with legislation.
- It may avoid the cost of tribunal procedures.
- It highlights the importance given to cultural diversity in the organisation and indicates that resources have been allocated to this as an important management activity.
- It provides a system which can be used to collect and monitor other equality data, as well as information relating to ethnic origin.

Checklist for action

- Inform all staff beforehand that information regarding ethnic origin is going to be collated. State clearly the reasons why this is being done.
- Be available to assist staff in completing the form if required.
- Make sure that you know what the information is to be used for and that you are in a position to respond to staff concerns regarding: purpose of collection; confidentiality of information supplied; what to do if ethnic origin is not clear to the individual.
- Be prepared to explain on an individual basis what the information is to be used for.

Pre-empting racial harassment in the workforce

Despite the UK's culturally diverse population, it is likely that, even in an organisation which has striven to remove obstacles to attracting and retaining a culturally diverse workforce, people from minority cultural backgrounds will still be in a numerical minority.

The establishment of a harassment policy is crucial in order to send a message to all staff that a minimum standard of behaviour is demanded in the workplace.

The drawing up of a policy, especially if it is carried out in consultation with staff, helps to send out a strong message of commitment from senior management.

A number of organisations, in order to implement the policy effectively, have set up networks of staff who have been trained to advise other staff who feel that they are being harassed.

Mentoring

Informal mentoring has been an integral part of organisational life for some time, and identified as part of the normal work experience of many managers. The advice and guidance which they receive through the informal network which exists both within and outside the workplace means that they have direct access at an early stage in their careers to information about how the organisation works; and to information about what will contribute to their progression at a later stage.

However, this advice and guidance is rarely available to the minority employee who does not necessarily mix informally with the majority group and therefore misses out on the opportunity to find out how things really get done, as opposed to what the formal structure of the organisation would indicate.

Developmental opportunities go to people who are already operating effectively within this network, to the exclusion of those who do not operate in that sphere. This very effective informal network (which is in fact very similar to a mentoring scheme) operates in many organisations, but only for people from a particular background, and often to the exclusion of others, such as staff from other cultural backgrounds, female staff and disabled staff.

It would be impossible to remove the informal mentoring which goes on, although that would be one way of equalising the situation for everyone and promoting greater cultural diversity. However, it has and continues to operate in a way which has positive outcomes for those within the network. So why not extend this 'scheme' to include others?

What are the benefits to the organisation of establishing a formal mentoring 'scheme' which embraces staff from the diverse cultural backgrounds working in the organisation? It has now come to be widely recognised that a flourishing and effective organisation is one that can call upon a range of talents arising from diverse experiences and backgrounds. If it is accepted that it is desirable to attract and retain staff from a variety of backgrounds it must be realised that mentoring is an effective way of facilitating their induction, enhancing their skills and developing their talents.

However, it must first be acknowledged that since people from minority cultures experience life in ways which may be qualitatively different from their white male counterparts in the apparently same situation, mentoring would need to be modified to suit their requirements. The assumptions may not apply about cultural norms, strategies needed to negotiate the organisational environment and understanding of corporate culture, inter-relationships, information and opportunities available and power basis in the organisation, which mentors bring to their task when dealing with a white male staff member.

Thus, the choice of the mentor becomes crucial if the staff member from a minority background is to benefit from the scheme to the same extent as the others in the organisation.

We will concentrate here on staff from minority cultural backgrounds, but the principles could transfer into numerous other applications in the working environment, for example for women, disabled staff, all new entrants, and so forth. The following chart indicates the stages to consider.

Mentoring programme

Identify need

1. Is there under-representation of minority staff, particularly at senior levels in the organisation?
2. Are minority staff grouped in particular sections and functions?
3. Is there a higher turnover among minority staff as opposed to other staff?

Draw up a strategy for the mentoring programme
Ensure that this is adequately resourced

Recruit mentors   Recruit mentees

Include: Include:
Selection criteria   Selection criteria
Networking   Induction

Allocate mentors to mentees

Establish reporting and monitoring mechanisms

Monitor and evaluate

Exercise: Benefits of a mentoring programme

What are the benefits of a mentoring programme designed for minority staff?

Benefits for the mentee	Benefits for the mentor	Benefits for the organisation

The authors' suggestions are shown on page 107.

Possible benefits of a mentoring programme:

For the mentee	For the mentor	For the organisation
Offers an opportunity to receive information from a role model in the organisation who has an interest in the mentee's success.	Increases own profile in the organisation. Senior management recognises the mentor's contribution to the organisation. Contributes actively to the change process in the organisation. Offers an opportunity to develop own coaching skills, thereby feeding into own career.	Provides a mechanism to tap into the potential of a part of the workforce which has previously been under-utilised. Offers a programme of high-quality development of the next generation of staff and managers. Retains senior minority staff and gives positive feedback to them and recognition of that contribution. Provides good external publicity for the organisation − indicates being an innovative company. Provides an initiative within the staff development programme which could be extended to other groups of staff.
Gives inspiration that it is possible to progress in the organisation.		
Increases self-confidence.		
Develops knowledge about how to progress in the organisation.		
Fulfils own potential within the organisation.		

Appraisal systems

It has become more popular in recent years to introduce formalised systems of performance appraisal into organisations. The aims of an appraisal system include assessing past performance and identifying development needs, potential and aspirations in order to enhance future performance against organisational objectives.

For the manager of a culturally diverse workforce, the challenge is to ensure that the system of appraisal which is selected gets the best out of staff from the different cultural backgrounds represented in the workforce.

Key elements of an effective appraisal system are:

- Leadership from the top
- Demonstration of commitment and implementation from the top
- Clarity of objectives
- Acting upon information gathered within an agreed timescale
- Careful introduction of the system, giving consideration to:
  —consultation with staff
  —possible resistance
  —overcoming barriers
  —reviewing and, if necessary, modifying the system to reflect the diversity of employees' cultural backgrounds
  —including equal opportunities issues as a performance indicator
  —training for appraisers and appraisees
  —procedures for monitoring.

Consideration of the following points will help the manager to run appraisals in a way which gives staff from all cultural backgrounds the best chance to perform in their own terms.

- Thinking about the fact that employees from different cultural backgrounds to one's own might work with a different set of assumptions, expectations and rules regarding appropriate behaviour with one's manager. For example, in one culture what may be a sign of being a 'high-flyer', for example asking for more responsibility and asking for a salary increase, may be perceived as pushy, rude and even a sign of insubordination in another culture. This then affects how the appraiser and appraisee perceive and evaluate each other.

- Effective communication of the aims of the appraisal system to all staff. It may be helpful to consider coaching individual members of staff to enable them to make full use of the appraisal interview.
- Implementation of periodic reviews during the year as well as the annual appraisal interview.
- Encouragement of staff to evaluate their own performance by considering how effectively they feel they have worked. In general terms, the feedback they have been receiving from people they come into contact with, and what their results have been against personal and organisational goals. All this could be noted in preparation for on-going and annual reviews.
- The extent to which individuals feel they are expected to detail their achievements — and to claim them as their own — varies from culture to culture. There should be clarity about what is required of both the appraiser and the appraisee; in particular what is required of them during the appraisal interview.
- Ensure that there is an opportunity in the appraisal for the appraisee to indicate factors which may have affected their performance. For example, lack of cooperation from colleagues or clients.
- Build in a system of feedback from the appraisee on their view of how the appraisal has been conducted.
- Often performance expectations and how performance is to be evaluated are not discussed between the manager and subordinate at an early stage in their employment. This can place the minority person at a particular disadvantage if they are not party to the unwritten codes of behaviour and performance in the organisation. Performance expectations

and how they are to be measured should therefore be made clear from the outset, with objectives mutually agreed.

- Because people can be stereotyped due to their cultural backgrounds, and this can result in appraisers unwittingly using subjective criteria, it is advisable that appraisals are clearly related to performance in the job. This helps both the manager and the employee have confidence in the system.
- Training for appraisers should include awareness-raising about how stereotyping can occur unintentionally, affecting the career progression of the individual. It should be highlighted that stereotyping could occur when evaluating past performance or future potential, and when giving guidance on possible future career paths.
- As appraisal is very much a two-way process, training programmes for appraisees which include practising the skills involved in performing in the expected way in the appraisal interview – for example, stating own needs and viewpoints – will help employees who have not acquired this guidance informally.

And finally, if the results of appraisal interviews are monitored centrally in the organisation, this can help to ensure equity of treatment to staff from all ethnic and cultural backgrounds.

Influencing others – contract compliance

The creation of a working environment in which all members of staff, from a variety of cultural backgrounds, can operate to their full potential is limited in effect if it relates solely to the organisation and its own internal policies and practices.

An increasing amount of business is being contracted out to other organisations or external consultants, on a fixed-term, freelance or project basis. The staff from the external contractors come into contact with the internal core staff of the organisation itself and with its customers.

It would therefore be contradictory, unhelpful and undermining, if the external contractors and suppliers were not equally committed to the principles of equality in the same way as the main organisation.

Some organisations have taken steps to integrate cultural diversity principles and practices into their agreements and contracts with external contractors and suppliers. This can take the form of a written contract or letter of agreement and the kinds of requirements include:

- Supply of written cultural diversity policy with the tender for the contract
- Supply of information regarding policy implementation of the contractor or external consultant
- Agreement about non-use of racist and sexist language
- Demonstration of what the policy means in practice to staff in the organisation
- Attendance at appropriate training as required.

An organisation relates to external organisations in a number of ways. It therefore has an influencing role with a wide range of other organisations.

Exercise
To promote cultural diversity at work with external organisations, it is necessary to consider the following:

Which external organisations/activities should an organisation be influencing?	How could this be done?

The authors' suggestions are shown on page 112.

To promote cultural diversity at work with external organisations, the following are some suggestions about what could be done:

Which external organisations/activities should an organisation be influencing?	How could this be done?
Suppliers	Include questions relating to cultural diversity in contracts drawn up with suppliers
Tenders	Request demonstration of diversity policies and practices in any tender for work from an external (or internal) tender
External consultants/trainers	Draw up an agreement with external consultants/trainers which requires them to adhere to your organisation's diversity policy
Caterers	Request equality monitoring information from external organisations, including caterers, to demonstrate their achievements in relation to staff

The following section relates to taking action. This is presented in three parts: first an exercise on action planning for the organisation, followed by a summary of the key steps to be taken, and then a personal audit for the individual to consider.

Organisational action planning

Ideas for evaluation and planning are grouped under the headings of policy, commitment, structure and practice.

For each of the following questions, note down in the appropriate column what you are currently doing and then what further steps you could take in your organisation.

Policy	Current situation	Actions points
1. Does your organisation have: • A diversity policy • Does the policy go beyond what is required under UK anti-discrimination legislation • A racial (and/or sexual) harassment policy • A staff training and development policy • A disciplinary and grievance policy? 2. Have these policies been disseminated to all managers and staff?		

Commitment	Current situation	Action points
1. Is the senior management team committed to the diversity policy?		
2. Has the senior management team been seen to demonstrate commitment to this policy?		
3. Have resources been allocated for its implementation?		

Structure	Current situation	Action points
1. Do you have an effective structure in place with powers invested in people to implement the policy?		
2. Do you have a network of racial (and/or sexual) harassment advisers?		

Practice	Current situation	Action points
1. Has your organisation devised a programme of action to turn the policies into practice?		
2. Do managers and staff have codes of practice or guidelines on the above policies?		
3. Has the organisation's publicity been evaluated with cultural diversity in mind? For example: ● marketing materials ● product/service advertisements ● job advertisements ● selection of culturally diverse group of staff to attend promotional activities, for example graduate recruitment fairs.		
4. Do you monitor your publicity and information brochures for the inclusion of positive examples – eg the inclusion of positive images of a culturally		

Practice	Current situation	Action points

diverse workforce and clientele?

5. Are the following informed about your policy:
   - staff
   - prospective clients
   - clients
   - contractors?

6. Has the organisation set itself equality targets for under-represented groups?

7. Are managers appraised on their performance in relation to diversity issues?

8. Do you have an employee monitoring system (data collected on ethnic origin, sex, age, family commitments, disability, religion, etc)?

9. Do you regularly evaluate and review the implementation of:
   - your diversity policy
   - your employee monitoring system?

10. Do you operate a job share scheme?

Practice	Current situation	Action points
11. Do you offer flexible working hours or other kinds of flexibility?		
12. Is the issue of promoting the benefits of a diverse workforce being addressed?		
13. Has managing diversity training been provided to the senior management team? If so, did it cover:		

- effective communication and consultation
- strategic planning and objective setting
- organisational culture and management of diversity
- spreading ownership of organisational diversity objectives
- recruitment/ appraisal/career development
- leading/ motivational skills
- discipline and grievance handling
- racial and sexual harassment?

Practice	Current situation	Action points
14. Is the issue of diversity included in your management development training?		
15. Are the following available to staff: • training for appropriate staff in recruitment and selection practices within six months of taking up post • diversity issues as a part of induction training • appropriate management development based on each individual's needs • assertiveness training according to individual need?		
16. Are exit interviews conducted and, if so, are issues relevant to the principles of diversity raised?		
17. Are job descriptions and method of advertising of job vacancies regularly reviewed, looking at issues such as: • links with local communities • positive action advertising?		

Practice	Current situation	Action points
18. Do you encourage support networks for all your staff?		
19. Do you have any programme of positive action training?		
20. Do you operate an across the board career break scheme?		
21. Do you run training for women returners?		
22. Do you offer childcare facilities?		
23. Are issues of diversity addressed in contracts with other organisations?		

Seven key steps towards successful management of a culturally diverse team

Step 1. Ensure that the organisation has a diversity policy
The policy should state the organisation's commitment to cultural diversity and highlight particular groups whom experience shows are more likely to be discriminated against, for example on grounds of culture, race, gender, disability, sexual orientation, or age.

The policy should be disseminated to all employees in the organisation.

Step 2. Ensure that the organisation has a policy on creating an environment which is free of harassment

This policy should give a clear definition of what harassment means, with examples of what the behaviour might be. The policy then needs to be communicated to all members of staff, with clear guidelines on how to proceed in the event of harassment.

It is important to set up a structure to support the implementation of the harassment policy. In the policy document it should be made clear who in the organisation has overall responsibility for the policy.

A formal and informal structure should be set up to respond to complaints of harassment. The formal structure should link to the grievance and disciplinary procedure. An informal network of harassment advisers, trained and supported by the organisation, form a useful first stage service to people who may perceive that they are being harassed, but would prefer to speak to someone informally and get advice rather than go through a formal procedure.

Step 3. Devise a structure to oversee the implementation of the policies

A structure appropriate to the organisation needs to be set up so that the policies are adequately supported. This could be in the form of a working group or committee, headed by a senior manager.

Step 4. Review current practices

Carry out a review of current practices in order to ensure that there is no direct or indirect discrimination in the following areas and that there is genuine access for all:

- Recruitment and selection
- Terms and conditions of employment
- Access to promotion
- Access to training opportunities
- Working hours
- Grievance and disciplinary procedures.

Step 5. Set up an ethnic monitoring system

The first stage is for the senior management team to decide what the information is going to be used for. Once that has been clarified, deciding what ethnic categories to use will follow. For example, if the purpose of the exercise is to measure the composition of the workforce against the ethnic breakdown nationally, or in the local catchment area, it would be useful to gather the information using the categories in the National Census 1991, namely:

- White
- Black Caribbean
- Black African
- Black other
- Indian
- Pakistani
- Bangladeshi
- Chinese
- Other Asian
- Other.

The staff should be asked for the information on a self-classification basis. If the information is requested under the signature of the chief executive this helps to achieve a higher response rate.

Action should be based on the monitoring data, for example targeted recruitment; contacts set up with a range of community organisations; schools and colleges liaison work; development of diverse publicity materials; targeted training and development programmes.

Step 6. Introduce a training programme on diversity for managers and staff

A range of training courses should be designed and offered to appropriate levels of staff. Examples include:

1. Diversity in recruitment and selection (for all staff involved in the recruitment process)
2. Equality and diversity awareness (for all staff)
3. Managing a diverse team (for all supervisors and managers)
4. Personal effectiveness at work
5. Management development programme.

Step 7. Set up a mentoring system

Whether or not this is appropriate will depend on the mix of the workforce.

Once there is a critical mass, with some representation of minority staff progressing or having progressed into middle management or senior management levels, it may be an appropriate point to develop a mentoring system. This would develop lower-grade staff in order to retain and encourage progress to more senior levels and help both to attract and retain a more culturally diverse workforce in the organisation.

Personal audit

Individual ability and commitment is key to developing good practice within a culturally diverse workforce. Consider the following statements to see if you can identify points where you may need to take action in order to develop your own knowledge and skills in this area.

Personal audit	Yes	No
Commitment		
1. I am committed to encouraging diversity in my workplace.	☐	☐
2. Staff in my organisation or team welcome the opportunity to work in a culturally diverse team.	☐	☐
Knowledge		
3. I am aware of the ethnic mix of people in my organisation or team.	☐	☐
4. My team members are aware of the principles of equality and diversity and how they translate into practice in each of their jobs.	☐	☐
5. I have received clear recruitment and selection guidelines based on sound equality and diversity principles.	☐	☐
6. I have received clear guidelines on dealing with harassment.	☐	☐

Consider those questions where your response is 'No', then consider what influence you have in your organisation or team to include these issues in your strategic planning on diversity.

Self-test: generating ideas for managing a diverse team

Under each prompt, list ideas as appropriate to your own organisation:

(a) Certain kinds of positive action in an organisation can help attract and retain staff. It can be done by:

Ideas _____

_____

_____

(b) Support systems are useful to help ensure that staff from culturally diverse backgrounds are retained. Methods to use are:

Ideas _____

_____

_____

(c) There are many barriers to implementing a diversity policy. These barriers include:

Ideas _____

_____

_____

(d) There are a number of benefits to having staff of different cultural backgrounds represented in an organisation. Some of these benefits are:

Ideas_____

_____

_____

(e) It is important to place a programme of cultural diversity within the broader context of diversity. What is the broader context of diversity?

Ideas_____

_____

_____

(f) It is important to place a programme of cultural diversity within the broader context of diversity. Why?

Ideas_____

_____

_____

The authors' suggestions are shown below.

Self-test: the authors' suggestions

Generating ideas for managing a diverse team. You may have listed the following:

(a) Certain kinds of positive action in an organisation can help attract and retain staff. It can be done by:

- Putting statements in job advertisements welcoming applications from the particular groups which are under-represented.
- Placing job advertisements in a more diverse range of newspapers and journals.
- Publication of the organisation's policies on diversity.

(b) Support systems are useful to help ensure that staff from culturally diverse backgrounds are retained. Methods to use are:

- Training and development programmes tailored to the needs of staff from a variety of cultural backgrounds.
- Development of support networks for a culturally diverse workforce.

(c) There are many barriers to implementing a diversity policy. These barriers include:

- Lack of clear commitment from the top of the organisation.
- Personal prejudices and stereotypes influencing decision-making.
- Resistance to new ideas and change.

(d) There are a number of benefits to having staff of different cultural backgrounds represented in an organisation. Some of these benefits are:

- Greater range of skills to respond to the needs of the clients.
- Wider mix of staff can attract a wider client base.

(e) It is important to place a programme of cultural diversity within the broader context of diversity. What is the broader context of diversity?

- Gender, disability, sexual orientation, age, trade union activities, political beliefs.
- Recruitment and selection; training and development; policy development.

(f) It is important to place a programme of cultural diversity within the broader context of diversity. Why?

- To break down the barriers which arise in discussing the sensitive issue of cultural diversity.
- To put the issue within the area of mainstream management.

Glossary

Asian. The term 'Asian' is used throughout to denote people whose origins lie in the Asian continent.

Black. The term 'black' is used throughout to denote people of African and African-Caribbean ancestry.

Genuine occupational qualification. Selection for a job on the grounds of race (and/or sex) is allowed in certain jobs where being of a particular race (and/or sex) is deemed essential – for example when the appointment of someone from a particular race and/or sex will give the best service to the client. An example would be a Social Services Department providing people of a specific racial group with personal counselling, where it may be considered best for the counsellor to be from a specific ethnic background and experience. Such recruitment is allowed for under the Race Relations Act 1976, Section 5 (2) (d) and the Sex Discrimination Act 1975, Section 7.

Majority ethnic. The term 'majority ethnic' is used to denote the majority ethnic group in terms of the UK, ie white UK origin.

Minority ethnic. The expression 'minority ethnic' is used throughout to refer only to members of minority ethnic groups in the UK context, ie all ethnic groups which are not of white UK origin.

Positive action. Encouraging applications from members of under-represented groups; special training aimed at encouraging under-represented groups to enter areas of work where they have previously been under-represented. Action aimed at getting as wide a selection of people as possible to take up opportunities with the organisation, but nevertheless requiring selection on the basis of merit.

Positive discrimination. Selecting a job applicant simply because of their ethnic origin and not on merit or ability to do the job – this would be unlawful discrimination under the Race Relations Act.

Preferential treatment. Treatment in terms of access to jobs or promotion which would give an advantage to either the majority ethnic or the minority ethnic group, to the detriment of the other group.

Racism. Beliefs and social processes which discriminate against others on the basis of their supposed different racial characteristics.

Tokenism. The practice of offering opportunities to individuals from minority groups not necessarily on the basis of merit but as representatives of ethnic groups. The intention is to give the impression that discrimination does not occur.

White. Used in the text to refer to people of white UK origin. Interchanges in this context with 'majority ethnic' which would sometimes read clumsily in the text.